N I C K F A

Worship through the seasons
Reflective Services for Lent, Holy Week and Easter

First published in 2001 by KEVIN MAYHEW LTD
Buxhall, Stowmarket, Suffolk IP14 3BW
Email: info@kevinmayhewltd.com

The material in this book first appeared in *No Ordinary Man, No Ordinary Man 2* and *To Put It Another Way.*

9 8 7 6 5 4 3 2 1

ISBN 1 84003 826 8
Catalogue No 1500461

Cover design by Angela Selfe
Typesetting by Richard Weaver

Printed in Great Britain

Contents

Foreword

Few issues are more contentious in the Church today than worship. Its importance, in the minds of many, far outweighs theological, doctrinal or denominational differences. For some, the very idea of straying from tried and trusted patterns is tantamount to heresy. For others, those patterns have become associated with lifeless formality and, in consequence, abandoned. Personally, I believe we must make room for both, respecting and building on tradition but at the same time being open to new ideas.

One such idea I experimented with during my ministry was using meditations, music and slides to bring out the meaning of Scripture. My aim was to engage the senses in a way that would capture the imagination of those participating in worship, breathing fresh life into old and familiar passages, and offering insight into the not so familiar. In time, the various meditations I wrote for such services found their way into print, under the title *No Ordinary Man*, from which much of the material in this compilation derives. Several books later, there came *No Ordinary Man 2*, which accounts for the rest of this collection.

My purpose in both volumes of *No Ordinary Man* was very simple – to encourage people to reflect on the person of Jesus. I did not set out to provide answers so much as to provoke questions; to get people asking: 'Who was this man?' 'What did he do?' 'Why did he do it?' Above all, 'What does he mean for me today?' Each meditation explored such questions from the perspective of particular biblical characters that met with Jesus, either in person or through his Spirit – people like Mary and Joseph, Simon Peter and Mary Magdalene, John the Baptist and Paul. The first part of both books comprised one hundred such meditations; the second gave outlines for services and Quiet Days.

This compilation brings together in one book the services and appropriate meditations for Lent, Holy Week and Easter from the two volumes of *No Ordinary Man*. Each service comes complete with suggested readings, meditations and prayers, together with suggestions for hymns, music and slides – you will need only to add intercessions and, perhaps, further prayers. If you want to make things simpler, you may choose to omit the slides and/or music, although doing this will inevitably diminish some of the impact. Alternatively, again, you may prefer to pick and mix, making use of some of the suggestions but using other ideas of your own.

When using slides and music, there are obviously certain basic requirements. A good hi-fi system, slide projector and screen are essential, as is an effective amplification system so that readers' voices carry over any background music. You will also find the services of an assistant invaluable when it comes to presenting the material – ideally somebody to control the slide projector, and possibly someone to fade the music in and out as appropriate. Remember, too, to ensure that those reading the meditations are given proper time to prepare beforehand, and that they are instructed to read slowly and clearly, beginning by announcing the title of the meditation.

You can probably borrow much of the recommended music from your local library or a friend. Should you prefer to buy it, much is available on budget CD sets. I made particular use of *The Voices of Angels (100 Heavenly Classics)*, *100 Romantic Classics*, *100 Relaxing Classics* and *100 Popular Classics* (Castle Communications); *Discovering the Classics* (three-volume double CD set), *Renaissance Choral Treasures* and *Classical Favourites for Relaxing and Dreaming* (Naxos) and the *Classic Experience*, discs 1 and 3 (EMI). Other works extensively used are Vivaldi's *Gloria*, Handel's *Messiah*, Mozart's *Requiem*, *Mass in C minor* and *Coronation Mass*, and a recent composition called *Fountain of Life*, written by Margaret Rizza and available from Kevin Mayhew Publishers Ltd.

Slide collections are not easy to find nowadays. You may be able to buy some from Rickett Educational Media Ltd (01458 253636) but many, sadly, are out of print. Your best bet may be to borrow them from your local Diocesan Resource Centre if you have one. Failing that, you might once more try your local library. When using slides always run through them beforehand, making sure they are the right way up and in the correct order. Make sure also that you have a spare bulb in case one should blow, and arrange all electrical leads so that no one can inadvertently fall over them. The less you leave to chance, the less possibility there will be of anything going wrong.

Organising a service of this kind undeniably takes time and effort but, in my experience, this is well worth putting in. It is very different from the style of worship people are used to, but perhaps because of this it may be able to bridge the gap between the diverse contemporary patterns and understandings of worship, and, more important, speak to those who may not usually contemplate attending church. If this book helps to open up a new dimension of worship that is able to speak to all, then it will have served its purpose.

NICK FAWCETT

Ash Wednesday

Suggested visual material Jesus of Nazareth 2 and 4
The Life of Christ II
The Gospel: Life of Jesus

Music *Intermezzo (Carmen, Suite No. 1)* Bizet

Introduction For many people Lent is associated with giving something up. It is seen as an opportunity, perhaps, for kicking that unwanted habit, for going at last on that long-intended diet, or for denying oneself those unnecessary extra luxuries. All such acts of discipline may have their place, but they give a very one-sided view of this season, for, if anything, it should be about taking something on; committing oneself, in the words of Jesus, to going the extra mile. That doesn't mean taking work on for work's sake. Rather, it is about resolving to follow Christ more faithfully, a determination to give him our wholehearted discipleship. It might mean more disciplined devotion, perhaps more practical service, maybe more effective witness, or possibly the offering of previously unused gifts. Whatever it is, it is more than giving something *up*; above all, it is giving something *back* to the one who gave us his all. Consider today what Christ has done for you; then ask what you can do for him, and use Lent as an opportunity to respond.

Hymn *O loving Lord, you are for ever seeking*
Take this moment, sign and space

Prayer

Living God,
forgive us that, too easily, we slip into a faith of negatives,
imagining that you are more concerned with what we shouldn't do
than with what we should.
Teach us that although there is a very real place for self-denial
there is also a place for affirming and celebrating life
in all its fullness.

Help me, then, to use this coming season of Lent
as a time to grow and learn,
to deepen my faith and strengthen my commitment;
above all, a time to make more time for you,
so that you can work in my life
and enrich my experience of your love,
through Jesus Christ my Lord.
Amen.

Hymn *O loving Lord, you are for ever seeking*
Take this moment, sign and space

Reading Matthew 5:13

Meditation of Peter
Salt.
You can't get much more ordinary than that, can you?
We've got masses of the stuff,
enough in the Dead Sea alone to supply the world's needs,
I shouldn't wonder!
So when Jesus turned to us the other day and told us,
'You are the salt of the earth'
you can well appreciate why I scarcely batted an eyelid –
it was hardly the highest accolade he could have given, was it?
At least, that's what I thought then,
only now I'm having second thoughts,
for it's struck me since just how much we use salt:
for preserving,
purifying,
seasoning,
even healing wounds on the odd occasion –
such remarkable properties for so commonplace a substance.
It's one of those things we take for granted –
until we haven't got it,
and then, suddenly, we realise how much it's needed,
how vital a role it has.
Is that what Jesus was saying to us –
that our role too, though in a different sense of course,
is to preserve and purify,
to bring a little extra sparkle and spice into life,
to help heal this bleeding broken world of ours?

Not in any pretentious way,
blowing our own trumpet or parading our virtues,
but quietly,
without fuss,
our contribution barely noticed yet indispensable nonetheless –
the world a poorer place without our service?
It's a thought, isn't it? –
inspiring,
daunting,
breathtaking,
humbling –
though it's hard to believe,
the idea of us making even half such an impact, quite frankly incredible.
Yet just imagine if we could,
what a ministry that would be!
And, come to think of it, isn't that precisely what we see in Jesus,
his life lived for others,
his way of unassuming service,
gently yet irrevocably transforming the world?
I was wrong, wasn't I?
For in that simple illustration
he paid us the highest compliment possible
and issued the most awesome of challenges.
'You are the salt of the earth' –
you can't get much more special than that, can you?

Silence

Prayer
Lord Jesus Christ,
we thank you for the difference you have made both to our own lives
and to the experience of so many people like us.
We thank you for the difference you have made to our world,
working through countless individuals
and transforming innumerable situations across the centuries.
You call us, in turn, to make a difference –
to help bring joy, hope and healing to those who are hurting,
all who have lost their sense of purpose or faith in the future.
Forgive us for so often failing to honour that calling,
our discipleship making such a feeble impact on those around us.
Teach us to reach out in your name
and to share in your renewing work.

Teach us to be salt of the earth,
 fit for use in your service,
 to the glory of your name.
Amen.

Hymn *There's a road which leads to Jerusalem*
Yesu, Yesu, fill us with your love

Reading Luke 19:11-27

Meditation of John Mark
Gifts?
Skills?
Talents?
Don't look at me,
 they're for others!
Believe it or not, I actually thought like that once,
 convinced that when it came to handing out his blessings
 God was running short when it came to me.
I'd wanted to do something,
 nothing I'd have liked more,
 but, in all honesty, what could I contribute to his kingdom?
The idea of me having any meaningful role was, to put it mildly,
 a non-starter!
All right, so there were a few jobs I could turn my hand to if pushed,
 but there were countless others infinitely more able,
 any number you could choose from more suited,
 more qualified than I would ever be.
No, I was quite happy to plod along in the background,
 to make up the numbers,
 be one of the supporting cast.
Maybe I wouldn't make any waves but I could live with that;
 we can't all be celebrities, can we? –
 and happily some of us don't want to be.
I'd have gone on believing that too, but for Jesus,
 for ever convinced I had nothing to offer.
Only that parable of his made me think again,
 helping me to understand that we all have some kind of gift,
 every one of us,
 if only we look hard enough –
 some great, some small,
 a few with many and many with few,
 but we *all* have something to contribute,

a talent we can use in the service of the kingdom,
and whether we do that is not an optional extra but a vital necessity,
a privilege and responsibility we dare not waste.
It may not be a show-stopper,
the sort of talent that catches the eye and attracts the plaudits,
but it's no less valuable for that,
no less worth cultivating,
for, used wisely, it can still make an impression at the right time
and the right place.
It's not what you've got that counts,
but what you do with it,
and we all have something we can offer, no matter how small it may be.
So enough of putting yourself down.
God has a job for you to do,
and he's depending on you to do it.
The results may surprise you.

Silence

Prayer
Lord Jesus Christ,
when it comes to others
we are often guilty of thinking too highly of ourselves,
puffed up with our own importance and thrusting ourselves forward,
but when it comes to you we can make the opposite mistake,
underestimating the gifts you have given us
and failing to appreciate all we can do with your help.
We see our weaknesses rather than strengths,
our limitations rather than potential,
the obstacles that confront us
rather than the opportunities waiting to be grasped.
Help us to recognise that you not only value us
but that you have given us all a gift or gifts to be used in your service,
a unique role as part of your body here on earth.
Teach us, therefore, to offer all we are
and everything we can do joyfully to you,
knowing that you can take it and use it
in ways that exceed all our expectations.
In your name we ask it.
Amen.

Hymn *Will you come and follow me?*
From heaven you came, helpless babe

Reading Mark 4:26-29

Meditation of Matthew

I thought it was down to me, the way he'd been talking.
For one awful moment I actually thought the dawn of the kingdom
hinged on *my* efforts,
my faithfulness,
my contribution to the cause.
What a frightening prospect!
Imagine what it would mean, were it true:
I'd be waiting for ever,
looking forward in vain expectation to a day I'd never finally see,
for, despite my best intentions, I'd be bound to fail –
I always do –
the job hopelessly beyond me.
Don't get me wrong,
it's not that I haven't a role to play –
we all have that,
each having something valuable to contribute –
but, thank God, his purpose is bigger than any one of us,
his kingdom growing as often as not despite rather than because of us!
Whether we see it or whether we don't, it's there slowly growing –
seeds starting to sprout,
shoots bursting into flower,
fields ripening for harvest –
God's hand inexorably at work,
refusing to be denied.
That doesn't excuse us, of course,
never think that.
We all have a responsibility to help it happen,
through word and deed to bring the kingdom closer,
and if we fail in either we may find ourselves excluded
when the day finally comes.
But that doesn't mean we must try and do everything,
bear the whole burden on our shoulders,
for we're in this together,
partners in faith,
dependent ultimately on God to take what we offer
and use it to his glory.
Take heart from that when progress is slow and your efforts seem in vain,
when the fulfilment of his promises seems further away than ever.
Never give up,

never lose faith,
for the kingdom has dawned and its growth is assured –
the final victory not down to us
but to him.

Silence

Prayer
Lord Jesus Christ,
it is hard sometimes not to feel overwhelmed
by the scale of the challenge facing us
and the obstacles that seem to block our path.
You call us to proclaim the gospel
but so few seem interested in hearing it.
You ask us to make disciples of all nations
but only a handful seem willing to respond.
We live in a world where faith is ridiculed
and your name casually dismissed,
a world in which people live for today with no thought of tomorrow
and in which good seems overpowered by evil.
Instead of truth we see falsehood,
instead of love, hatred,
instead of peace, division,
instead of joy, sorrow,
the dawn of your kingdom apparently further away than ever
rather than drawing near,
and we feel powerless to do anything about it.
Teach us, despite everything, not to lose heart.
Help us to understand that we have a part in your purpose
but that the final victory is down to you.
Give us strength simply to do what you ask of us as best we can
and to leave the rest in your hands,
confident that, though we may not see it,
the seed you have sown is growing,
and the day will come when your kingdom will be established
and you will rule with the Father,
one God, world without end.
Amen.

Hymn *Here I am, wholly available*
Lord Jesus, we must know you

Reading Luke 10:25-37

Meditation of the lawyer who questioned Jesus

'Teacher,' I said, 'what must I do to inherit eternal life?'
and I knew what he was going to say, even as I put the question.
It was typical of the man's genius,
somehow always turning the tables on those who tried to catch him out.
And this time was no exception.
'What is written in the law?' he asked. 'What do you read there?'
Brilliant!
Only this time he would meet his match,
for, unlike others, I was ready for him,
all set to turn the tables back again and put him firmly on the spot.
So I played along, confident of emerging on top.
'Love God,' I said, 'love your neighbour.'
It was the answer he'd been looking for,
and he nodded with a smile of satisfaction,
as though that was that,
the discussion at an end,
the issue resolved:
'Do this and you will live.'
But that was my cue,
and I leapt in gleefully,
sensing the kill.
'Yes,' I smirked, 'but who is my neighbour?'
Clever, don't you think?
And I genuinely believed I had him stumped,
one masterly stroke exposing the fatal flaw in his reasoning.
You see it sounds reasonable enough, doesn't it? –
'love your neighbour as yourself' –
the sort of commandment none of us would want to argue with,
never even presume to question,
but what does it actually mean?
If you've never asked yourself that then it's high time you did,
for perhaps then you'd be a little less keen on the idea,
a little less prone to let the words trip so lightly off the tongue.
Why?
Well, quite simply, how wide do you spread the net?
How far do you go before finally drawing the line?
The people next door, are they your neighbours?
Or is it those in your street, your town, your country,
those who share your creed, or colour, or culture?
Where does it start?

Where does it end?
You tell me.
And that's the question I put to Jesus,
  fully expecting him to flounder
  as he tried to extricate himself from my trap.
Come on, I reasoned, there had to be limits somewhere!
The Romans, for example,
  our hated oppressors –
  he couldn't mean them for a start.
Nor tax-collectors, prostitutes and sinners,
  you could write them off for certain –
  accept them and we'd be talking of Samaritans next, God forbid!
So how about our enemies,
  those who persecute, insult and accuse us falsely –
  don't tell me we're meant to love them too?
Preposterous!
No, I had him pinned down,
  his back to the wall,
  and there could surely be no escape?
Only then he looked at me,
  and told that unforgettable story about, you've guessed it . . .
  a *Samaritan!* –
  and somehow the question was once again back where it started,
  with *me:*
  'Which of these three was a neighbour to the man?'
I realised then with a stab of shock
  and a sense of disbelief,
  that he meant it,
  that he seriously wants us to treat everyone, everywhere,
  as our neighbour,
  Jew and Gentile,
  slave and free,
  male and female,
  rich and poor –
  no person outside our concern,
  no situation we can wash our hands of.
I'd put the question,
  I'd had my answer,
  and, I tell you what:
  I wish I'd never asked!

Prayer
Lord Jesus Christ,
we feel overwhelmed sometimes when we realise
what you are asking of us,
when we begin to reflect on what is involved in Christian discipleship.
Your words concerning love for our neighbour sound so wonderful
until we stop to ask what they mean,
and then, suddenly, the scale of the challenge,
the enormity of our responsibility
and the likely cost of service dawns on us
and we wonder how we can ever cope.
Fill us with your love so that we may love in turn.
Give us your spirit of humility and self-sacrifice,
and equip us to reach out in your name, putting others before ourselves.
Teach us what it means to belong not just to the community of faith
but to the family of humankind,
and in serving them may we serve you also,
to the glory of your name.
Amen.

Hymn *Lord, as we rise to leave this shell of worship*
Go forth and tell!

Blessing

Music *Intermezzo (Carmen, Suite No. 1)* Bizet

First Sunday in Lent

Suggested visual material
Jesus of Nazareth 2
The Life of Christ II

Music
Comfort ye my people (Messiah) Handel

Introduction
We are here in the season of Lent; a time that calls us to stop, take stock and reflect on the health or otherwise of our faith. It recalls the temptation of Jesus in the wilderness, and invites us to consider our own response to temptation in turn. It reminds us of his steadfast commitment to the way of the cross, and asks if we are willing to bear the cost of discipleship. It speaks of the prayer and devotion that sustained Jesus during those forty days and nights of testing, and from there urges us to make time and space for God a priority in our own lives. Today we listen to some of the accounts of that time in the desert, exploring what it meant for Jesus, what it meant for John the Baptist, and what it means for us today. We look back, asking that God might lead us forward.

Hymn
When he was baptised in Jordan
O love, how deep, how broad, how high

Prayer

Loving God,
we try to look at ourselves openly and honestly,
but we find it so hard,
for we are so often blind to our faults,
closed to anything that disturbs the image
we have of ourselves.
So we come to you,
appealing to your grace and mercy.
Search us, we pray –
forgive us our sins,
cleanse us of our iniquities,
have mercy on our weakness,

and through your love create a clean heart
and a right spirit within us.
Remake us,
redeem us,
restore us,
and grant that we may live as your people,
a new creation in Christ,
to the glory of your name.
Amen.

Slides and music

O thou that tellest (Messiah) Handel, during which Mark 1:9-13 is read

Meditation of John the Baptist

It took me by surprise, I don't mind admitting it,
his going off into the desert like that
the moment after his baptism.
You see, I thought that was my role,
to fulfil the words of the prophet –
'A voice crying in the wilderness:
"Prepare the way of the Lord."'
And I'd done it well,
patiently,
faithfully,
determined to play my part, come what may.
They'd come in their thousands,
flocking out to me like there was no tomorrow –
to be baptised,
to confess their sins,
to await the Messiah.
They were ready and waiting,
eager to receive him,
hungry for his coming.
And at last we saw him,
striding down into the water,
his identity unmistakable –
not simply Jesus of Nazareth,
but the Deliverer,
the Son of God,
the Saviour of the world!
I was ecstatic, you can imagine.

It was like a dream come true,
the answer to all my prayers.
And as he came up out of the water
I was waiting for the next move,
wondering what would follow.
I'm not quite sure what I expected,
but something dramatic at the very least –
a bolt from heaven perhaps,
a fanfare of trumpets,
a raising of the standard,
I don't know –
but some sign,
some symbol to let us know beyond all doubt
that the moment had come,
the waiting was over,
and the kingdom was here.
Only what did he do?
Well, like I say, he disappeared.
No pep talk,
no message for the crowd,
just off and away without so much as a backward glance,
and no hide nor hair of him seen for weeks afterwards.
To be frank, I was annoyed at first,
for it all seemed such an anticlimax,
but on reflection I can't blame him,
for I think it took *him* by surprise as much as it did *me*.
When I recall now how he looked
coming up out of the water after his baptism,
so joyful,
so radiant,
almost as though he'd heard God rather than me talking to him,
I just can't believe he had any idea
that minutes later he'd be making off into the wilderness.
It was like he had no say in the matter,
as though an unseen hand was guiding him,
so that the one event progressed naturally from the other –
a moment of joy –
a time of trial;
a wonderful high –
a desperate low,
a certainty of faith –
a wrestling with doubt.

Yet by all accounts it's been the making of him,
almost as if faith needed to be forged on the anvil of temptation,
tested to the limit
before the weight of the world could be hung upon it.
I think I'm beginning to see it now,
to understand that it wasn't just the wilderness of Judea
he faced out there,
but the desert of the soul,
and he needed to experience both if God was to use him,
for, strange though it may seem,
God is often more at work when we don't see it
than when we do.

Silence

Slides and music

Mars (The Planets) Holst, during which Luke 4:1-13 is read

Meditation of the Devil

I thought I had him.
Not just once but three times
I thought I'd caught him out,
stopped him in his tracks before he'd barely had time to get started!
And I was close,
even *he*, I expect, would give me that.
Oh, he started off well enough –
sure of his destiny,
confident of his ability to grasp it.
But then he would have, wouldn't he,
coming out into the wilderness like that straight after his baptism,
heart still skipping within him,
the memory fresh,
the voice of God ringing in his ears.
But forty days on –
forty days of gnawing hunger, desert heat and night-time chill –
and then it was a different story,
hard then to think of anything but the pain in his belly
and the simple comforts of home.
So I saw my chance,
and made my move.
Nothing crude or clumsy –
no point scaring him off unnecessarily –

just a subtle whisper,
a sly suggestion:
'Turn this stone into bread.'
And he was tempted, don't be fooled.
I could see by the gleam in his eyes and the way he licked his lips
that, if you'll pardon the expression, he was chewing it over.
It wouldn't have taken much to make him crack, I'm certain of it;
one whiff of a fresh-baked loaf
and I'm sure he'd have given in –
why didn't I think of it!
Only then he remembered those cursed scriptures of his,
and all my hard work was undone in a moment:
'One does not live by bread alone.'
It was a setback,
but I pressed on, confident I was making ground.
And soon after he was up on the mountains,
the world stretching out before him as far as the eye could see.
'All this is yours!' I whispered.
'Just forget this Messiah business and grab it while you can.'
Oh, you may sneer with hindsight at my methods,
but it's worked before,
many a lofty ideal sacrificed on the altar of ambition.
But not Jesus –
not even a suggestion of compromise:
'It is written, "Worship the Lord your God, and serve only him."'
So I took him in his imagination up on to the temple
and played my trump card:
'Go on,' I urged him, 'Throw yourself off.
If you are who you think you are, God will save you,
for *it is written*:
"He will command his angels concerning you, to protect you.
On their hands they will bear you up,
so that you will not dash your foot against a stone."'
A master-stroke, so I thought,
quoting his own scriptures at him like that,
and, let's face it, we all like a little reassurance, don't we,
however strong our faith;
the knowledge, should the worst come to the worst,
that there'll be someone to bail us out when we need help?
'Why should he be any different?' I reasoned –
he was as human as the next man,
as vulnerable as the rest of your miserable kind.

But, somehow, even then he held firm:
'It is said,' he answered,
'"Do not put the Lord your God to the test."'
Well, that was it,
I knew I was beaten.
There was nothing left to throw at him,
so I slithered away to lick my wounds.
But I'll be back, you mark my words,
and next time, when it's his whole life in the balance,
a question of do or die,
then we'll see what he's really made of, won't we?
Then we'll see which of us is finally the stronger.

Silence

Hymn *Forty days and forty nights*
O changeless Christ, for ever new

Slides and music

And the glory of the Lord (Messiah) Handel
during which Luke 4:14-15 is read

Meditation of John the Baptist

He was back at last!
After countless days of silence,
no sight nor sound of him,
suddenly he was back where he belonged
and taking the world by storm.
It was a relief, believe me,
for I'd begun to wonder what I'd done,
whether I'd somehow put my foot in it,
even got the wrong man.
You see, he'd come to me there in the Jordan,
and I'd thought immediately, 'This is the one,
the Saviour God has promised,
the lamb that takes away the sin of the world!'
And what an honour,
what a joy for me, John, to baptise him,
to be there at the beginning of the Messiah's ministry,
the inauguration of God's kingdom!
Only then he disappeared,
without trace,

the last I saw of him making off into the wilderness,
alone.
What's going on, I wondered?
Where's he off to?
I wanted him back here at the sharp end where he was needed –
wasn't that what he'd come for –
to bring light into darkness,
joy out of sorrow,
hope in despair?
But he was gone,
and as the days passed with no word,
no sign,
no news,
so the doubts began to grow.
Had I misunderstood,
presumed too much?
Had I caused offence,
given the wrong signals?
I wondered,
and I worried,
day after day my confusion growing,
and I'd all but given up hope,
ready to write the whole business off as some sad mistake,
when suddenly he was back,
the word spreading like fire,
his name on every tongue –
Jesus of Nazareth,
preacher and teacher,
the talk of the town.
I still don't know what he got up to out there,
why he needed to spend so long out in the desert,
but it doesn't matter any more,
for he's here now where we need him,
and he's come back stronger and surer,
almost as though the wilderness
meant as much to him as his baptism,
if not more!
Does that make sense to you?
It does to me.

Silence

Slides and music

Canticle de Jean Racine Fauré, during which Luke 7:18b-19, 21-23 is read

Meditation of John the Baptist

Shall I tell you something strange?
Almost funny you might call it, were it not so sad.
It's about me,
the voice in the wilderness,
the baptiser in the Jordan,
the one sent to prepare the way of the Lord.
Well, I managed that, didn't I?
Or at least so they'll tell you –
I made straight a path in the wilderness,
I paved the way for his coming,
and, yes, I have to say I made a good job of it,
too good in a sense,
for, much to my embarrassment, many were so impressed
they followed me instead of him.
But it wasn't just them who got it wrong,
it was me,
for when Jesus finally came I was as unprepared as any.
Oh, I didn't realise it at the time,
far from it –
in fact, I thought I was an example to them all,
the one who, more than any other,
understood who he was and what he came to do.
'Behold the lamb of God!' I told them,
'the one who comes to take away the sin of the world.'
A good speech, wouldn't you say?
But it was just words,
sounding impressive,
but belying the truth beneath.
And it wasn't long after –
when his ministry had begun and mine ended,
when he was travelling the byways of Judah
and I was rotting in prison –
that I found myself questioning everything.
'Could he be the Messiah?' I asked,
'the one we'd so long waited for?'
If he was, then why was so little happening –
why so little evidence of his kingdom getting closer?
I should have known different, of course I should,

and, yes, you may well say a hint of jealousy
coloured my judgement.
But, honestly, how would you have felt in my position,
knowing that, having given your all,
more would be asked,
even life itself?
It won't be long now before they come for me,
I'm under no illusions.
There's no escape,
no possibility of a last-minute reprieve;
that wife of Herod's won't rest
until she sees me dead and buried,
the voice in the wilderness silenced for ever.
I wasn't prepared for that when I started,
and I still wouldn't have been, just a day ago.
But God has given me time to think,
to hear what Jesus is doing,
to understand what it's all leading up to,
and I'm ready now,
at last I'm ready,
prepared for anything,
prepared for everything!

Silence

Prayer

Gracious God,
deal mercifully with us, we pray.
Give us the courage we need
to see ourselves as we really are,
the faith we need to see ourselves as we can be,
the wisdom we need to discern your will,
the humility we need to accept your correction,
and the commitment we need
to respond to your guidance.
We know our faults,
we recognise our need for help,
and so we come to you,
dependent on your grace.
Gracious God,
have mercy,
in the name of Christ.
Amen.

Hymn *It is a thing most wonderful*
Lord Jesus, for my sake you come

Blessing

Music *Lord of my life (Fountain of Life)* Rizza

Second Sunday in Lent

Suggested visual material

Jesus of Nazareth 2 and 4
The Life of Christ II
The Gospel: Life of Jesus

Music

Allegro from *Spring (The Four Seasons)* Vivaldi

Introduction

'Be still and know that I am God.' How often have we heard those words? More important, how often do we make time to be still? Like Martha, all too easily we spend our lives rushing around, always aware of something else to do, something else that demands our time and attention. We live in an ever more pressurised world in which time to stop and stare has become an all too rare luxury. But Lent reminds us that we fail to make time for what really matters at our peril. It calls us to pause and reflect. It challenges us to ask what life is ultimately all about. Today then we make a space in our lives, and through music, through words, through slides and through silence, we seek to make sense of it all. 'Be still and know that I am God.'

Hymn *Seek ye first the kingdom of God*

Prayer

Living God,
it's easy to fool ourselves
that we are observing Lent –
giving up certain vices,
denying ourselves particular pleasures,
making bold resolutions.
It's easy to imagine this is what Lent is all about –
but it's not.
For Lent above all is a time for reflection,
for self-examination,
for prayer,
for renewed commitment.

We come then today to reflect,
to search ourselves,
to seek your guidance,
to offer you our love.
Help us through this service to hear your voice,
and to be strengthened in the service of Christ.

Slides and music

Domine Fili unigenite (Gloria) Vivaldi, during which Mark 8:27-33 is read

Meditation of Peter

It was a wonderful moment,
I really thought I'd cracked it.
After all the uncertainty,
all the questions,
all the confusion,
I finally believed I understood who he was.
'You're the Messiah!' I told him,
and he beamed at me with such delight that I felt my heart would burst.
No one else had grasped it you see,
not properly.
They wondered, of course,
but like so many others they were still guessing,
groping in the dark.
He might as well have been Elijah or John for all they realised.
I was different, and Jesus knew it.
'Blessed are you,' he said, 'for God has revealed this to you and not man.'
What an accolade!
But then it all went wrong,
just when I felt I'd arrived the bubble burst,
and with a vengeance!
I suppose I got carried away,
never stopped to think.
Typical of me, really.
It's just that it came as such a shock,
him going on like that about the future,
everything he had to suffer,
all doom and gloom,
even talking of death itself.
I wasn't having any of it.
'Not likely!' I shouted. 'No way!'

I meant no harm,
  I just didn't think such things could happen to the Messiah,
But you should have seen his face,
  the anger, the disappointment.
Satan, he called me!
Can you believe that?
Me, his right-hand man,
  the one who'd just hit the nail on the head,
  the pick of the bunch, so I thought –
  Satan!
I was hurt at the time,
  cut to the heart if I'm honest,
  but I can see now, all too clearly, that he was right and I was wrong.
I still had so much to learn,
  so much to understand,
  and I needed a reprimand, a stern hand, if I was to progress any further.
I'd only just begun to glimpse the truth
  and if I'd have had my way
  it would have meant him denying everything he stood for.
He *was* the Messiah but not in the way *I* meant it;
  he *had* come to establish his kingdom,
  but in a very different way than *we* expected.
His was the way of service, of sacrifice, or self-denial,
  offering his life for the life of the world.
I see that now and I marvel at his love,
  but what I marvel at even more is that
  even when I understood him so little
  he understood me so much.

Slides and music

And the glory of the Lord (Messiah) Handel
during which Mark 9:2-3 is read

Meditation of John

It was fantastic,
  extraordinary,
  mind-blowing;
  a once-in-a-lifetime experience,
  and I was lucky enough to be there –
  me, and Peter and James up on the mountain with Jesus.
We knew something was going to happen;

we could see it from his manner when he asked us to join him,
but we never dreamt of anything like that.
He seemed to change before our eyes,
his clothes to glow,
his face to shine.
And then – would you believe it –
who did we see with him but Moses and Elijah!
Clear as day they were,
chatting together like old friends.
We were struck dumb for a moment,
lost for words,
and then dear old Peter got stuck in as usual.
'Can I do something?' he blurted out,
'You will stay, won't you?'
And why not?
I mean, we were all enjoying ourselves,
didn't want the moment to end,
almost too good to be true!
But strangely, as soon as Peter finished speaking,
the spell seemed to break.
The sky darkened as clouds came over
and then, as a peal of thunder broke the silence,
Moses and Elijah disappeared,
leaving Jesus standing there alone,
looking just as he always had,
as ordinary as you or me.
Did we imagine it?
We've often asked ourselves that.
Or was it a vision,
brought on perhaps by the heat
or the altitude,
or simply having one too many before we set off?
It must have been something like that, surely?
There's no other logical explanation.
Yet it's funny how we all saw the same thing,
all down to the last detail.
I don't know what to make of it,
but I wouldn't have missed it for the world.
It helped me understand what Peter had already begun to grasp,
that Jesus was the Messiah,
the answer to all our prayers,
the fulfilment of the Law and the Prophets.

It was just a glimpse,
a moment's wonderful insight
which I thought at the time could never be repeated.
And that was true in a sense,
for no one will ever witness quite what we saw in the way we saw it.
But we have all seen his glory now,
not just the three of us,
but Thomas, Andrew, Mary, Matthew, and so many others –
the glory of the Father revealed in him.
We see it day after day after day,
full of grace and truth,
And, believe me, that too is fantastic,
extraordinary,
unforgettable!

Silence

Meditation of Peter

I wanted to hold on to that moment for ever,
to keep things just as they were for the rest of eternity,
for I feared life would never be so special again.
It was just the four of us –
well, six if you count Moses and Elijah, but I'm not sure you can do that –
the four of us sharing a blessed moment of peace and quiet;
no crowds pleading for a miracle,
no lepers begging for healing,
no Pharisees baying for his blood,
no Sadducees spoiling for a fight.
Just us,
together,
as we'd all too rarely been.
And we knew it couldn't last;
he'd made that perfectly clear when I dared suggest otherwise.
There was trouble round the corner,
his enemies waiting to pounce,
and he knew it was only a matter of time before they got him.
Not much of a prospect, was it –
rejection, suffering, death?
I don't know how he stuck it, I really don't.
But we didn't want to think about such things,
not then anyway,

and up there on the mountain it all seemed a million miles away,
out of sight, out of mind.
Can you blame me for wanting to stay,
for wanting to hang on to the moment for as long as possible?
Only I couldn't, of course.
You can't stop the clock, can you, and make the world stand still?
You can't store those golden moments safely away,
untarnished by the march of time.
Life goes on, as they say,
and you have to go with it,
like it or not.
It was hard to accept that,
hard to go back to the daily round
with its familiar demands and expectations.
Yet as I spoke to Jesus, coming down the mountain,
I realised suddenly it had to be;
that there was no other way –
going back, I mean.
Without that there would have been no point,
those sacred moments an empty illusion.
He knew that,
and slowly, very slowly, I came to know it too.
It was a vital time, a special time,
one that gave him new strength,
new resolve,
the inspiration he needed to face the future and fulfil his destiny.
But it was as much for us as for him
a moment we could look back upon,
so that afterwards we might keep on looking forward.

Silence

Hymn *Christ upon the mountain peak*
Father, hear the prayer we offer

Slides and music

Chanson de Matin Elgar, during which John 4:1-7 is read

Meditation of the woman at the well

He was full of surprises, that man,
from the moment I first met him.

I thought he'd just push me aside like all the rest;
either that or walk away with his head in the air.
He was a Jew, remember, and I a Samaritan;
and worse than that,
a woman,
alone.
Yet he stayed where he was, a smile on his face,
quite happy, apparently, to be associated with me.
Well, call me suspicious if you like, but I wasn't sure what he was up to,
so I asked him straight out, 'What's your game?'
He laughed at that, and then offered me a drink of water –
at least I thought that's what he was doing, though I wasn't sure.
You see, he had no bucket,
and he could hardly shin down the well, could he?
So where was this water he was on about meant to come from?
To be frank, I suspected he was pulling my leg,
but I was beginning to like him despite the nonsense he talked.
He had a nice way with him:
kind,
gentle,
a bit of all right in an unconventional sort of way.
So I played along, wondering where it would all lead.
If only I'd known –
what an embarrassment I might have saved myself.
I'll never know how he guessed,
but suddenly he looked straight at me
and for the first time I noticed his eyes.
They didn't undress you like so many men's seem to do,
but looked much deeper,
almost as if into my very soul.
And then he started talking about my lovers,
my husbands,
my past,
every detail correct.
It was uncanny,
frightening,
far too near the knuckle,
So I tried to fob him off with some old chestnut about worship.
But even then he threw me;
none of the usual pat answers
but a response that reached right to the heart of the matter,
cutting through all the trivia.

And then he produced the biggest surprise of all –
told me he was the Messiah!
I didn't know what to say,
just stood there gawping, flabbergasted.
I mean, I realised he was a prophet,
but the Messiah?
It couldn't be, I told myself,
no way.
I went back down to the village, seeking reassurance,
wanting someone to tell me he was just another religious nutcase.
But they didn't.
They were curious,
wanted to see for themselves.
And when they heard him,
listened to his teaching,
they believed he was the Messiah.
Me? I still don't know, but I wouldn't be surprised,
not if I'm honest;
nothing would surprise me about him.

Slides and music

Chi Mai – Ennio Morricone, during which Mark 10:13-16 is read

Meditation of Andrew

I could have brained those children,
rushing around like that with their yelling and shrieking,
shattering our peace and quiet.
We'd had him alone at last,
just us and Jesus;
a rare opportunity to sit and listen undisturbed,
drinking in his every word.
And it was wonderful,
a truly magical moment,
until, that is, they turned up –
those wretched kids ushered forward by their doting parents,
just so that he could touch them.
Really, how ridiculous!
Superstition, that's all it was –
no real faith behind any of it –
just sentimental rubbish,
nauseating!

So we tried to stop them; you can understand that, surely?
We wanted to get back to the business in hand,
  before we were so rudely interrupted;
  back to more serious matters.
OK, so maybe we were a bit over the top,
  a touch more heavy than the situation demanded,
  but we were angry,
  disappointed.
I mean, could *you* have concentrated with that row going on?
I couldn't.
Yet did they care?
Not likely!
We fully expected Jesus to back us up,
  send the lot of them packing.
But can you believe this? He didn't!
He actually turned on us,
  and there was anger in his eyes,
  anger touched almost with pity.
'Leave them alone,' he said. 'Let them come to me. What's your problem?'
Well, we didn't know what to say, did we?
It caught us right on the hop.
So we just fidgeted uncomfortably, trying to cover our embarrassment.
It was so unfair.
We'd meant no harm, after all,
  certainly hadn't meant to upset anybody;
  yet there they were now,
  the kids bawling their eyes out,
  the mums looking daggers at us,
  the dads having a go at everyone –
  what a mess!
I honestly didn't know what to do next.
But thankfully Jesus came to the rescue as always.
He reached out and took the children in his arms, one by one,
  a great loving hug.
And then he lifted them up for all to see.
'These are special,' he told us,
  'More precious than you will ever know –
  each one treasured by God.'
And you could tell from the way he smiled at them,
  and the way they smiled back at him,
  that he meant every word he was saying,
  and they knew he meant it.

I still feel a bit aggrieved by it all –
well, you can tell that, can't you?
But I realise now we made ourselves look rather silly that day,
even childish, you might say;
and I'm beginning to understand Jesus has no room for the childish,
only the childlike.

Slides and music

Aria from *Bachianas Brasileiras* Villa-Lobos
during which Luke 10:38-42 is read

Meditation of Mary, sister of Martha

I felt sorry for Martha, I really did;
she was doing her best after all.
Someone had to see to the hospitality,
make sure the dinner was all right,
wash up after us,
and, to be honest, I felt I wasn't pulling my weight.
I could see she was getting harassed
despite the smile she kept on her face.
She didn't say anything, but she didn't need to,
I could tell by the way she looked that she was angry.
And with good reason.
It was selfish of me,
unforgivable,
but I couldn't help myself.
He was so fascinating,
so easy to listen to,
so genuine.
It was as though every word he spoke was for me,
answering the questions I'd never dared to ask,
meeting the needs I never even knew existed,
giving me the sense of purpose I had so longed to find.
How could I get up to wash dishes?
Interrupt him to offer another drink?
It would have been sacrilege.
I knew I might never have another chance like that again,
and so, shame on me, I sat back and let Martha get on with it.
I wasn't surprised when she finally complained,
but I was by the answer Jesus gave her.
I expected him to back her up, give me a ticking off –
after all, fair's fair.

But instead he praised me
  and rebuked her!
He spoke gently, of course,
  almost tenderly,
  yet it was a rebuke for all that.
I don't know how she felt but I could have died of embarrassment.
It was my fault, you see –
  me who effectively earned her that reprimand –
  and I expected her to be furious afterwards;
  I know I would have been.
Yet funnily enough she wasn't.
She was very quiet for a time,
  very thoughtful,
  and then she told me not to look so guilty,
  for Jesus had been right.
He'd made her face herself for the first time,
  and she realised now she couldn't go on running for ever,
  couldn't go on hoping being busy would disguise the emptiness inside.
She'd been made to stop and ask herself what life was all about,
  and in Jesus she had begun to find the answers.
She's still the efficient hostess, of course,
  always will be.
And me?
  I'm just as ready to find an excuse for laziness given half the chance!
But we've changed, both of us,
  grown closer,
  found inner contentment,
  become more at peace with ourselves,
  because through meeting Jesus we've each discovered what really counts,
  the one thing we really need.

Silence

Prayer
Loving God,
  we think we are so busy, so pressurised,
  having so much to do.
We rush around day after day with never a
  moment to spare.
Yet so often we forget the one thing we really need –
  to make time and space in our lives to meet
  with you,

to hear your voice,
and to look at the world from your perspective.
Loving God, teach us to be still
and to know your presence.

Hymn *Father I place into your hands*

Blessing

Music Allegro from *Spring (The Four Seasons)* Vivaldi

THIRD SUNDAY IN LENT

Suggested visual material
Jesus of Nazareth 3, 4 and 5
The Life of Christ II
The Gospel: Life of Jesus

Music
Come to me (Fountain of Life) Rizza

Introduction
Who was Jesus? What lay at the heart of his message? Why had he come? What did it all mean? These and a host of other questions must have teemed in the minds of all those who glimpsed anything of the earthly ministry of Jesus. No one who heard his words or witnessed his actions could have been untouched by the experience, for here was a man who spoke and acted with an authority no one has ever matched. The result may have been more questions than answers, as much rejection as acceptance, but one thing is clear: when people came into contact with Jesus they had to decide for themselves just who it was they were dealing with; there could be no sitting on the fence. And as we listen today to words of Scripture and reflect upon the encounters they record, the same challenge is put to us: what do we make of this man and his message?

Hymn
Jesus, name above all names
Love divine, all loves excelling

Prayer

Lord Jesus Christ,
we remember today how the crowds
listened spellbound to your teaching,
how they gazed in wonder
as you demonstrated your love in action,
how they gave thanks to God
as you transformed the lives of all
who came to you seeking your help.

Come again to our lives,
  to your Church,
  and to your world today.
May your power be seen,
  your love displayed,
  your forgiveness received
  and your word proclaimed.
Break through the complacency of our discipleship,
  and fire us with renewed commitment,
  restored vision
  and revitalised faith,
  so that we may live to your glory,
  and lead others to a saving knowledge of your love.
For your name's sake we ask it.
Amen.

Slides and music

Träumerei Schumann, during which Matthew 5:38-45 is read

Meditation of a listener to the Sermon on the Mount

Can you believe what he told us?
'Love your enemies', that's what he said!
Pray for those who abuse you,
  and if someone slaps you in the face, turn the other cheek!
Well, I ask you, what sort of talk is that?
He's on another planet, this fellow –
  cloud-cuckoo land!
Oh, it sounds wonderful, granted,
  but can you see it working?
I can't.
No, we have to be sensible about these things,
  realistic.
We'd all like the world to be different,
  but it's no use pretending, is it?
'Love your enemies' –
  where will that get us?
They'll see us coming a mile off!
And as for 'turn the other cheek' –
  well, *you* can if you want to, but not me;
I'll give them one back with interest –
  either that or run for it!

I'll tell you what, though,
we listened to him,
all of us,
just about the biggest crowd I've ever seen,
hanging on to his every word,
listening like I've rarely known people listen before.
Why?
Well, you could see he meant what he was saying for one thing –
the way he dealt with the hecklers and cynics:
never losing his cool,
never lashing out in frustration,
ready to suffer for his convictions if that's what it took.
He practised what he preached,
and there aren't many you can say that about, are there?
But it was more than that.
Like it or not it was his message itself;
that crazy message,
so different from any we'd ever heard before –
impractical,
unworkable,
yet irresistible.
It gave us a glimpse of the way life could be,
the way it should be –
and he actually made us feel that one day it might be!
No, I'm not convinced, sad to say –
life's just not like that –
but I wish it was.
I wish I had the courage to try his way,
the faith to give it a go,
for we've been trying the way of the world
for as long as I can remember,
and look where that's got us!

Silence

Slides and music

Intermezzo (Carmen, Suite No 1) Bizet
during which Matthew 6:31-33; 7:7-11 is read

Meditation of another listener to the Sermon on the Mount

'Ask,' he said, 'and you will receive.'
Just like that,
   or so at least it sounded.
As though all we have to do is put in our request,
   place our order,
   and at the drop of a hat it will be there before us,
   served up on a plate,
   exactly to our requirements.
Do you believe that?
I'm not sure I do.
And I'm not sure I want to either,
   for if he really meant that,
   then where would it all end,
   when could we ever stop asking?
We couldn't, could we?
Not while there's still suffering in the world,
   still need,
   sorrow,
   hunger,
   disease,
   despair.
It wouldn't be right –
   a dereliction of duty, you might call it.
And anyway, even if we could wipe those out,
   rid the world of its many ills,
   that wouldn't be the end of it, not by a long way,
   for there would always be something else to ask for –
   a gift we know we lack,
   a dream still unfulfilled,
   a person we long to reach –
   always just one more favour
   before we could be completely satisfied.
It would end up with God at our beck and call,
   bowing to our every whim,
   dancing to our tune, instead of us responding to his.
So no, he couldn't have meant that, could he?
But what then?
What was Jesus getting at
   with that weird but wonderful promise?
I've wrestled with that day after day,
   and I've begun to wonder

if maybe we're looking at it the wrong way round,
too much at self and too little at Jesus.
'Do not worry about your life,' he told us,
'what you will eat or what you will drink,
or about your body, what you will wear.
Strive first for the kingdom of God and his righteousness,
and all these things will be given to you as well.'
Ask for what matters, isn't that what he was saying –
for those things in life which can bring you lasting happiness –
treasures in heaven rather than pleasure on earth?
It's not that this life was unimportant to him.
He cared about the world's suffering
more than anyone I've ever known.
But he came to tackle not simply the symptoms but the cause,
not just the way things look but the way they are –
the way we think,
the way we speak,
the way we act,
each transformed deep inside.
I may be wrong, of course,
but I think that's what he meant;
something like it anyway.
Ask God for guidance, strength, faith, renewal.
Ask him to teach, use, shape, forgive you.
Ask for these things,
earnestly,
honestly –
the gifts of his kingdom –
and you *will* receive
until your cup runs over!

Silence

Hymn *Seek ye first the kingdom of God*
Yesu, Yesu, fill us with your love

Slides and music

He was despised and rejected (Messiah) Handel
during which Matthew 13:54-58 is read

Meditation of a resident of Nazareth

Do you know what they're saying about him?
You're not going to believe it!
There are all kinds of rumours flying about –
that he's Moses, Elijah or another of the prophets –
but some are now actually claiming he's the Messiah,
the one we've waited for all this time,
God's promised deliverer!
I said you wouldn't believe it, didn't I?
Yet plenty do, apparently,
a great multitude always around him,
hanging on to his every word,
applauding his every action,
following his every move with open adulation.
And the worst of it is he's done nothing to discourage them,
no attempt whatsoever to cool their ardour a little
or prompt a moment's reasoned reflection.
I'd swear he's coming to believe what they're saying about him,
allowing the hype and hysteria to go to his head –
at least that's how it seemed the other day
when he strolled back here into Nazareth,
entourage in tow.
Barely back five minutes,
and there he was in the synagogue
interpreting the scriptures,
telling us how we should live our lives,
as though he was an expert or something,
privy to some special relationship with God denied the rest of us.
Well, he may have fooled others,
but he didn't fool us –
no chance of pulling the wool over *our* eyes.
We've watched him grow up, you see,
followed his progress
from when he was a bundle in his mother's arms,
and we knew exactly who we were dealing with.
Oh, he'd always been a nice enough lad, I'm not denying that,
never any trouble like some I might mention,
but he was just an ordinary young man,
Jesus the carpenter's son,
from the back streets of Nazareth,
a local boy with, let's face it, dubious origins to put it kindly.
No, I won't go into that,

hardly fair to stir up old dirt,
but you get my drift, don't you?
We knew all about this man the crowds were flocking to,
and, frankly, the idea of him being sent by God was laughable.
The proof was in the pudding,
for what did he actually do here when it came down to it? –
precious few of those signs and wonders
everyone was raving about –
and, quite frankly, after all the hullabaloo
we felt he was a bit of a let-down.
It's strange, though, for no one else has said that,
not to my knowledge, anyway.
I hear fresh reports about him day after day,
and always it's the same story –
healing the sick,
cleansing lepers,
even raising the dead.
Funny he couldn't do it here.
There must be an answer somewhere, mustn't there?
Probably right under my nose if only I could see it.
But it's no good – we know the truth, don't we?
We've seen it with our own eyes,
so, whatever else, the fault can't lie with us.
It can't, can it?

Silence

Slides and music

Nocturne in B flat minor Chopin, during which Mark 12:28-31 is read

Meditation of the Scribe

He made it all sound so easy,
so simple.
The whole Law,
everything we'd been struggling to understand
for so many years,
summed up in two little commandments:
you shall love the Lord your God
with all your heart and mind and soul;
you shall love your neighbour as yourself.
It sounds perfect, doesn't it?

What our faith is all about – in a nutshell.
And for the most part I agreed with him –
 spot on!
Love God,
 love your neighbour;
 I've no problem with that –
 it's what I've tried to do all my life.
But love your neighbour as yourself –
 that's where I come unstuck;
 for though you may not believe it,
 and though it may rarely seem like it,
 I don't love myself at all.
Oh, I give a good impression, I know –
 I'm as selfish as the next person,
 invariably putting *my* interests before others,
 more often than not wrapped up in my own affairs –
 I can't deny that.
But beneath the facade,
 whenever I have the courage to look deep inside,
 I'm ashamed of what I see,
 ashamed of what I am.
Love myself?
With all my weakness,
 all my greed,
 all my pride?
You must be joking!
Only he wasn't, that's the mystery;
 there was no irony from Jesus when he said those words,
 no sarcasm,
 no hidden agenda.
Love your neighbour as yourself, he told us,
 and he meant it;
 he actually believed that I was lovable.
I just can't tell you what that means,
 what hope it gives me –
 him to say such a thing of all people!
For he was under no illusions,
 no false sense of my worthiness.
He knew me as I was,
 better than anyone,
 with all my faults,
 all my ugliness,

yet he still believed I was worth something.
Am I convinced?
Well, not as much as I'd like to be,
for there are still times when I look at myself
and turn away in shame.
I'm not pretty,
not special,
not a nice person at all when you get down to it.
But I've begun to understand that inside this stranger I call me,
beneath the mask I put on for the world,
there's a person who God truly values,
an individual unique and precious to him,
and if *he* believes that, despite everything,
who am *I* to argue?

Silence

Slides and music

Credo (Mass in B minor) J. S. Bach, during which Mark 9:14-24 is read

Meditation of the father of the epileptic boy

Lord, I do believe,
truly.
Despite my doubts,
despite my questions,
I do believe.
Not that my faith is perfect, I'm not saying that –
there's still much that puzzles me,
much I'd like to ask you about further, given the chance.
But I believe you're different,
that you can change lives in a way others can't,
that you can bring hope where there's despair,
joy where there's sorrow,
peace where there's turmoil,
love where there's hate.
And I need those things now as never before,
not for myself, but for my son.
He's suffering, you see,
troubled in body and mind,
day after day thrown into terrible convulsions.
And, Lord, I'm afraid of what might happen,
what he might do to himself when the fits come upon him.

It's breaking my heart seeing him like this,
having to stand by helpless as he writhes and groans.
Yet I've tried everything –
every doctor,
every healer,
even your own disciples,
all to no avail.
Not one has been able to help,
none able to provide the answer I long to find.
So I've come finally to you,
my last throw of the dice,
and I'm begging you, Lord:
help!
Oh, I know I don't deserve it –
I'm not pretending otherwise.
I have my doubts, all too many –
barely understanding half of what you teach,
and even what does make sense is hard to accept.
I don't have the makings of a disciple, I realise that,
all kinds of things wrong in my life –
ask anyone.
And though I want to change,
to become the person you would have me be,
I'm not sure I can come anywhere near it.
In fact, though I say I believe,
I'm not even certain of that,
for I'm torn in two,
half of me sure, half of me not,
my faith and doubt warring together,
each battling for the upper hand,
each ebbing and flowing as the mood takes me.
Yet I've seen what you've been able to do for others,
I've heard about the wonders you perform,
and I'm sure that if anyone can help me, then it's you.
So you see, I do believe a little,
not as much as I'd like,
not as much as I should,
but I do believe,
and I'm trying so hard to believe more.
In the meantime, I'm begging you, Lord,
on bended knee, I'm begging you:
help my unbelief.

Prayer

Loving God,
  we do not know all there is to know,
  or understand all there is to understand,
  but one thing we are sure of:
  that in Jesus Christ we have met with you,
  experiencing your love,
  rejoicing in your mercy,
  receiving your guidance,
  thrilling to your blessing.
There is much still to learn
  and much that will always be beyond us,
  but we have seen and heard enough
  to convince us of your grace,
  and we have tasted sufficient of your goodness
  to know that nothing can ever separate us
  from your love revealed in Christ.
Help us to live as he taught us,
  to love as he urged us,
  to serve as he showed us
  and to trust as he told us.
So may we live in him and he live in us,
  to the glory of your name. Amen.

Hymn *Let there be love shared among us*
Let there be peace on earth

Blessing

Music *Jesus, you are the way (Fountain of Life)* Rizza

Fourth Sunday in Lent

Suggested visual material
Jesus of Nazareth 2 and 4
The Life of Christ II
The Gospel: Life of Jesus

Music
Love's Theme from *Midnight Express*

Introduction
All too often, even today, we hear the comment 'It's a man's world', and, despite all the efforts of recent years to overcome discrimination, there is still some truth in that remark. Yet if that's so today, it was all the more so in the days of Jesus; women then in countless ways treated as second class citizens. For some the fact that Jesus chose only men to be his Apostles shows that even he was influenced by the attitudes of his day, but this is to overlook the important place he gave to women throughout his ministry, time and again making it clear through words and actions that women counted to him just as much as men.

Today, on this Mothering Sunday, we look at some of those women whose lives were touched by Jesus. We consider their faith, their personal experiences, their courage, their convictions. Listen to their testimony, for the Christ who accepted them is the same Christ who accepts us today – Christ who values all people equally and welcomes all into his kingdom.

Hymn *O loving Lord, you are for ever seeking*
Take this moment, sign and space

Prayer

God of peace,
quieten our hearts
and help us to be still in your presence.
We find this so hard to do,
for our lives are full of noise and confusion,
a host of demands and responsibilities

seeming to press in upon us from every side,
consuming our time and sapping our energy.
We run here and there,
doing this and that,
always something else to think about,
another pressing matter
demanding our attention –
and then suddenly,
in the middle of it all,
we stop and realise we have forgotten you:
the one we depend on to give us strength
and calm our spirits.
God of peace,
we offer you now this little space we have made
in the frantic scramble of life.
Meet with us,
so that we may return to our daily routine
with a new perspective,
an inner tranquillity,
and a resolve to make time for you regularly,
so that we may use all our time more effectively
in the service of your kingdom;
through Jesus Christ our Lord.
Amen.

Slides and music

Silent, surrendered (Fountain of Life) Rizza
during which Mark 5:25-34 is read

Meditation of the woman who touched Jesus' cloak

I was sick –
sick of body,
sick of mind,
sick of spirit –
fed up with having my hopes raised only to be dashed again,
fed up with everything.
I'd suffered for so long,
my strength failing,
my fears multiplying,
and I was ready to give up,
to say goodbye to it all,
to curl up in some dark corner and let life slip away.

But then suddenly I saw him, just a few yards in front of me,
the man they were all talking about –
Jesus of Nazareth,
prophet,
teacher,
worker of miracles –
and it took only one glance to convince me
he was the answer to my prayers.
Yes, I was desperate, admittedly,
ready to believe anything, clutch at any straw,
but there was more to it than that,
for I could see immediately that this man was unique,
everything about him proclaiming his love for others.
So I pushed my way through the crowds
and I reached out and touched him,
just the faintest of contacts, that's all,
yet immediately I felt whole again,
a knowledge deep within that I was well.
But before I had time to celebrate I froze in horror,
for he stopped,
and turned,
and looked around curiously,
eyes sweeping over the crowd.
Goodness knows how he'd felt my touch amongst so many,
but he had,
and I realised then the awfulness of what I'd done,
breaking every commandment in the book
by touching him in my condition.
I waited for the rebuke,
the explosion of anger which would shatter my illusions,
yet it never came;
just that one simple question:
'Who touched me?'
There was no escape.
Much as I longed to melt away into the crowd,
I knew there could be no deceiving this man,
so I shambled forward and blurted out the whole story,
pleading for forgiveness,
begging him to make allowances.
I still feared the worst,
but finally I dared to meet his eyes,
and there he was,

gently returning my gaze,
a look of love and understanding which I shall never forget.
'Daughter,' he said, 'your faith has made you well.
Go in peace, and be healed of your disease.'
It was true, the disease had gone,
but there was more than that,
much, much more.
I'd found new meaning, new hope, new purpose,
strength that I'd never known before,
peace such as I'd never imagined possible.
He sensed my need that day before I even expressed it,
responding instinctively to my silent plea;
and I'm whole now –
whole in body,
whole in mind,
whole in spirit –
ready for whatever life might bring,
ready for anything!

Silence

Slides and music

Lord of my life (Fountain of Life) Rizza, during which Mark 7:24-30 is read

Meditation of the Syrophoenician woman

Was he just testing me?
I'm still not sure even now,
but I think he must have been.
How else can you explain his reaction when first I approached him,
the very last thing I expected,
out of character with everything I'd been told of the man.
Aloof, some have put it, trying to put things kindly –
detached,
curt,
matter of fact.
But that wasn't how I saw it, not at the time anyway –
rude more like,
heartless,
dismissive.
To be frank, I could have burst into tears on the spot.
But I didn't –
I couldn't afford to, could I? –

my hurt counting as nothing beside my daughter's health,
and she needed help from this man
whether he liked it or not.
So I stuck at it,
protesting my case,
and persistence paid off,
the change in his attitude immediate and remarkable.
Your request is granted, he told me,
just like that –
no messing,
no strings attached –
just that simple response, and it was done!
She was healed,
my little daughter well again,
her spirit tranquil,
her mind at rest,
body and soul made whole, just as he'd promised me.
But why then that initial response,
so cold, so cruel, so callous?
Why put me down only to lift me up?
Was he just testing me?
In part he was, I'm sure,
his way of ensuring that my faith was real
and my commitment total,
yet I've come to believe it was more than that,
for I've considered since the message he shared
and the wonders he performed,
the life he lived and the love he showed,
and I see there a man whose concern was to break down the barriers
that keep us apart,
to heal our divisions and make us one.
He saw the faith I had,
the resolve,
the dedication,
and he used that to test not just me
but the crowds that thronged about him,
to show them that his love wasn't simply for the few,
as they seemed to imagine,
but for everyone,
even an undeserving Gentile like me!

Silence

Slides and music

Libera me Domine (Requiem) Verdi, during which John 8:2-11 is read

Meditation of the woman caught in adultery

I expected him to condemn me like all the rest,
to shake his head in disgust and send me to my death.
Just another self-righteous busybody, that's what I thought –
you know the sort,
the kind always up on their soap box,
sounding off about something or other,
telling folk how they ought to live their lives.
Not that it mattered much this time who he was,
for there was no getting away from it, I'd broken the law,
caught, as they say, well and truly in the act –
no way anyone could get me out of that one,
even if they'd wished to.
And you could see from the smug look of the Pharisees
that they felt the same –
lips twisted with contempt,
eyes glittering with hatred,
their hands positively itching to pick up the first stone
and strike me down.
It was just a matter of time,
a question of completing the necessary formalities
before the verdict was given.
So I cowered there trembling,
waiting for the fateful signal for them to begin,
expecting each moment to be my last.
I waited . . .
and I waited . . .
sweat trickling down my brow,
limbs shaking in terror . . .
But it didn't happen,
no word,
no sign,
nothing.
What could it mean?
A reprieve?
Surely not.
But what then?
Some heartless trick to prolong my agony,

an unforeseen last-minute technicality,
or simply a pause while they gathered the rocks to stone me?
There was only one way to find out,
so I looked up,
tense,
fearful . . .
then stopped,
transfixed,
catching my breath in astonishment,
for we were alone,
just the two of us,
me and Jesus,
not another soul to be seen.
I thought I was dreaming for a moment,
either that or the stoning had despatched me
unbeknown to another life.
But then he spoke,
his eyes gentle yet piercing as he voiced my unspoken question:
'Woman, where are your accusers?'
They were gone, each one of them,
none able, apparently, to throw the first stone;
and even as I struggled to take it in, he spoke again,
those marvellous, memorable words:
'Neither do I condemn you.'
I should have danced for joy, shouldn't I? –
whooped with delight,
laughed in exultation –
for I was free,
not simply reprieved but forgiven,
invited to go back and start again.
But I didn't laugh.
I broke down in tears,
the sobs convulsing my body,
tears streaming down my face,
for suddenly, faced by this astonishing man,
I saw myself as I really was . . .
and became my own accuser.
I'd expected death, and been given life,
feared judgement, and been shown mercy;
what had seemed the end was suddenly a new beginning –
and it was all too much to take in!
Not any more, though.

I understand now what he's done for me,
and I look back still to that day with wonder,
my whole being throbbing with praise,
for he met me in my need and made me whole,
he saw me at my worst,
and dared to believe the best!

Silence

Hymn *I know not why God's wondrous grace*
I am trusting you, Lord Jesus

Slides and music

Kyrie eleison (Fountain of Life) Rizza, during which Luke 21:1-4 is read

Meditation of the widow at the treasury

I was ashamed, if I'm truthful,
desperately praying that no one would notice me,
for what would they think
when they saw those two miserable coins of mine;
what sort of person would they take me for?
They seemed little short of an insult,
worse, in some ways, than bringing nothing at all,
and believe me, I'd toyed seriously
with staying away altogether to spare my blushes.
It had been different once,
when my husband was alive –
then I could hold my head up in any company,
my gifts, if not extravagant, were more than generous.
But times were hard,
a matter of getting through from one day to the next
as best I could;
life's little luxuries a thing of the past,
and many of its necessities too.
Yet there was one thing I was resolved to do, come what may,
even if it meant going short,
and that was to continue offering something to God.
So there I was, that day in the temple,
surreptitiously bringing my feeble gift.
It wasn't much, I know,
not in the eyes of the world, anyway,

but to me it was a small fortune,
the last thing I had in the world.
Well, you can imagine my horror when I arrived there
to find this crowd with Jesus watching.
It was my worst nightmare come true,
my pathetic offering exposed to the full glare of public scrutiny,
and I felt certain I would die of shame,
waiting with weary resignation
for the inevitable howl of laughter or snort of disgust.
And when Jesus nodded towards me
I could feel the colour rising to my cheeks,
skin crawling with embarrassment.
Yet then, he spoke,
his words, would you believe, not of condemnation but praise,
singling me out as an example to follow
rather than an object of ridicule.
It's the thought which counts, we sometimes say,
and Jesus understood that.
Somehow he knew how much that gift had cost me,
and to him those small pieces of copper
were like nuggets of gold!
I went out that morning with my heart singing,
head held high after all,
and I brought my offering from then on
without any hesitation or any sense of unworthiness,
for I understood that God sees things differently from us,
that he measures the gift not by how much it's worth,
but by how much it means!

Silence

Slides and music

Jesus, you are the way (Fountain of Life) Rizza
during which Mark 14:3-9 is read

Meditation of the woman who anointed Jesus' head

Was it guilt that made them turn on me?
I couldn't help but wonder,
for there were some there who'd welcomed me very differently
the last time I saw them,
eager not only to share my company but my bed as well.

Oh yes, there were a few skeletons in the cupboard that day,
  enough to wreck many a career and destroy many a family.
Is that what they thought –
  that I'd come to tell all,
  expose them for the hypocrites they were?
It would have served them right if I had.
But no, they had nothing to fear,
  such revelations were the last thing on my mind.
I wanted to see Jesus, that's all,
  for I'd come to recognise that here was a man
  different from any I'd known before,
  concerned not for himself but for others,
  his only desire, it seemed, to bring a little light
  into the darkness of this world.
I'd taken some convincing, mind you –
  the kind of man I was used to made cynicism come easy –
  but I'd watched him talking with the multitude,
  healing the sick, comforting the distressed;
  I'd seen him welcoming the poor, embracing the little children,
  accepting the unacceptable;
  and I knew then, beyond all doubt,
  that he was genuine through and through,
  offering a glimpse of the way life could and should be.
Quite simply I was entranced,
  captivated,
  longing to discover that life for myself.
I had no right to be there, I knew that,
  but I wanted to respond,
  to show him that he'd touched me
  in a way no one else had ever done –
  not my body but my soul –
  so I burst in with my perfume,
  ignoring the gasps, the protests, the cries of outrage,
  and in a wild impulsive gesture I poured it over his head,
  anointing him with love.
You should have seen their faces!
I actually think some thought I was making a pass at him.
But not Jesus –
  he understood –
  the compassion in his eyes as he looked up at me,
  the concern, the welcome,
  sending a tingle down my spine,

for these told me in a way words never could
that he had time for me,
time for the person I was
as much as the person I could become.
It cost me something that day,
not just the perfume but my career,
for there was no way I could carry on selling my body
after that encounter,
but I've this horrible feeling that Jesus is going to pay far more
for the love he has for us,
for as he leapt to my defence that day he said the strangest of things,
words which have troubled me ever since –
something about anointing his body for burial.
Could he really have meant it?
He's too good for this world, I've always said that,
but surely no one could want to remove him from it,
not even his enemies.
No one would want to do that –
would they?

Silence

Prayer

Lord Jesus Christ,
you spoke,
and you brought hope, joy, comfort, forgiveness;
you touched,
and you brought love, peace, healing, wholeness.
Come now,
and speak again,
bringing your word of life
into our parched lives and our weary world.
Come now,
and reach out again,
bringing your touch of love to our aching hearts
and to all who cry out for help.
Where there is despair, sorrow, hurt or guilt,
may your voice renew.
Where there is loneliness, turmoil, pain and sickness,
may your hand restore.
Lord Jesus Christ,
you came once,

you shall come again,
but we ask you: come now,
and bring your kingdom closer here on earth.
We ask it in your name.
Amen.

Hymn *Will you come and follow me?*
From heaven you came, helpless babe

Blessing

Music *Intermezzo (Carmen, Suite No. 1)* Bizet

Fifth Sunday in Lent

Introduction

Why do you think people followed Jesus in such numbers throughout his ministry? Was it the things he said or the things he did, the power of his words or the attraction of his deeds? The answer, of course, is both and neither. Take either the words or deeds on their own and, while they would have caused a stir, their impact would soon have faded, there being nothing to back them up or give them substance. But put them together and you have an irresistible combination; an example of a truly integrated life in which faith was expressed in action and reinforced by actions in turn. What Jesus said, he did, and what he did made sense of the things he said. For us there will always be a gulf between the two but it is a gulf we must do our best to cross if we hope to be effective in our mission. Unless we are seen to live up to our principles, and until we *show* the love of Christ as well as *talk* of it, our message will fall on deaf ears. When the two speak with one voice, then we will find him speaking through us.

Hymn *We are called to be God's people*
The Church of Christ in every age

Prayer

Loving God,
you promised Abraham that all the world
would be blessed through his offspring
and in Jesus Christ you fulfilled that promise.
You spoke through the prophets
of a Saviour who would redeem the world,
and in his coming those words were realised.
You declared that you would put a new heart
and a new spirit within us,
a chance to begin again,
and through his death and resurrection
that fresh start became real.

Throughout history
  you have not simply spoken of love,
  you have showed us what it really means;
  you have not merely talked of forgiveness,
  you have demonstrated mercy
  beyond anything we could ask for.
Help us, in turn, to prove our love for you
  through concrete actions,
  to show the sincerity of our faith
  by practising what we preach,
  to express our gratitude for your great goodness
  by committing ourselves to your service.
Teach us, through who *we* are,
  to witness to who *you* are,
  to the glory of your name.
Amen.

Reading Matthew 5:14-16

Meditation of a listener to the Sermon on the Mount

Had he made a mistake?
I thought he must have, at first.
'*You* are the light of the world'?
It had to be wrong, surely?
That was *him* wasn't it, not *us* –
  he the one who brings light to those walking in darkness?
At least that's what I'd always believed,
  that one day God would send a Messiah
  whose glory would shine like a beacon in the world,
  all nations drawn by his radiance
  and nothing able to overshadow the brightness of his coming.
So what was *this* all about,
  turning the tables on us
  so that suddenly *we* were the ones called to be light,
  we those with the responsibility of scattering the darkness?
It was the last thing I expected,
  and the last thing I'd bargained on,
  for I knew that on my own I could scarcely raise a flicker,
  let alone a light bright enough to bring glory to God.
If it was down to *my* efforts,
  my faith,
  then there'd be no hope for anyone, would there?

And, of course, he knew that, as much as anyone.
It's *his* grace that floods our souls,
his love that fills our hearts,
his light that shines in our lives,
and without that we can do nothing.
But that doesn't mean we can simply sit back and leave it all to him,
for alongside what he has done for *us*
faith is about what we can do for *him*!
It involves giving as well as receiving,
serving as well as being served,
and we need to do that not simply when the mood takes us,
but every day, every moment,
the call at the very heart of discipleship –
the essence of faith.
The light of the world –
yes, it means *you* as well as him,
for though ultimately *he* is the true light,
the one who illuminates the way for all,
he needs *your* love,
your deeds,
your compassion,
your faith translated into action
if the darkness is not to close in and his light be obscured.
'Let your light shine before others,
so that they may see your good works
and give glory to your Father in heaven.'

Silence or Hymn *Lord, the light of your love is shining*
Father, whose mighty word

Reading Matthew 7:24-27

Meditation of a listener to the Sermon on the Mount

It's a great picture, isn't it?
A wonderful, almost ridiculous, contrast!
The wise man building his house on sure foundations
and the fool building his on the sand.
Could anyone be so stupid?
You wouldn't have thought so, would you?
And I was confident of one thing:
you wouldn't catch me making such a mistake,
not the slightest danger of that at all.

No, I understood that there's more to life than meets the eye;
more than money or material possessions, status or success,
for none of those are certain when the going gets hard
and the storms break over you.
I knew there had to be something else,
and in Jesus I thought I'd found it.
As I listened to his teaching and marvelled at his ministry,
as I saw for myself lives transformed,
broken, battered individuals healed, renewed, forgiven,
I decided that here was what life is all about,
and I rejoiced in his message of love and forgiveness.
I drank in his every word,
determined to make the blessings he spoke of mine,
confident of experiencing the joys of his kingdom.
Only then it came, just as he'd warned it would do –
the rain fell,
the floods rose,
the wind blew and beat against me –
and, with a sickening crash, I fell.
That's right, you heard me,
I fell!
Why?
Because I thought I'd obeyed, and I hadn't,
I thought I'd been wise, and I'd been a fool,
I thought I'd listened, and I'd barely heard,
ignoring the one thing that really mattered.
'Everyone,' he said, 'who hears these words of mine
and acts upon them
will be like a wise man who built his house on rock.'
I'd done the first but not the second,
the faith I professed all words and no actions,
and now, when the moment came, I was found wanting,
life crumbling into the sand after all.
I'd come close, yet not close enough,
recognising that Jesus was the way, the truth and the life,
but accepting it only with my head,
not my heart.
Don't make my mistake.
Don't sit back believing you've done all that needs doing,
or, like me, you may be in for an unwelcome surprise.
It's not hearing his words that matters,
not even accepting they are true;

it's whether they make a difference to who you are,
whether they change the way you live,
whether you hear and act upon them.

Silence or Hymn *The Church's one foundation*
How firm a foundation

Reading Luke 16:19-31

Meditation of a modern-day aid worker

It could never happen now, could it?
Is that what you tell yourself
when you read these stark and shocking words?
Nobody today could be so cruel,
so callous as to gorge themselves senseless
while some poor wretch lies dying of hunger on their doorstep.
The world has changed –
more caring than it used to be;
even the most selfish of people have some kind of conscience,
some sense of responsibility towards others.
And yes, if we're talking of those we can see,
those literally on our doorstep,
perhaps you're right –
I say, *perhaps*.
But the world has changed in other ways too;
our neighbour is not just the one down our street,
but across the world,
in every country and continent.
The refugee struggling wearily to the makeshift camp in search of shelter,
the starving child, eyes wide in mute appeal,
the elderly couple, barely more than skin and bone,
the broken mother, weeping over her lifeless little one –
these are the poor man at our door,
longing for a crumb to fall from our table.
The victim of drought,
the family made homeless by flood,
the people displaced by war,
the nation oppressed by debt –
these are the ones whose cries reach out to God
even while our prayers fall on deaf ears.

Make no mistake,
this was no idle tale,
no cosy illustration of the virtue of charity.
This was Jesus laying it on the line,
presenting the challenge fair and square,
setting out in black and white what God requires,
and warning us of the consequences should we fail to heed it.
Is it different today?
Of course it is,
for there are thousands, millions, crying out for help,
clamouring for justice,
and we can't meet all their needs no matter how we try,
not by ourselves, anyway.
But while we feast on our riches,
a multitude go hungry,
while we thank God for his provision,
a world asks what became of their share.
It's time to take Jesus seriously,
to listen to his question and face up to its challenge.
Are we doing enough?
Are we doing anything?
You tell me.

Silence

Prayer

Gracious God,
we thank you for all those
who reach out in your name,
all who seek to express your love
and concern for the needy in action –
those who bring food to the hungry,
healing to the sick,
homes to the homeless,
justice to the oppressed;
all who work for a better world,
a more just society,
a more caring planet.
Inspire us to support their work
in whatever way we are able,
whether through the giving of our money,

the offering of our prayers,
the commitment of our time
or the deployment of our service.
And stir us also through their example
to respond in our turn,
showing our care and compassion,
our love,
our commitment to you
through our commitment to others.
May we too make known your love,
in word and deed,
to the glory of your name.
Amen.

Hymn *God's Spirit is in my heart*
Father of glory, whose heavenly plan

Blessing

Palm Sunday

Suggested visual material
Jesus of Nazareth 5
The Life of Christ III and IV
He Carries our Cross (a)

Music
Gloria in Excelsis Deo (Gloria) Vivaldi

Introduction
Palm Sunday is one of the enigmas in the Christian calendar. It speaks of joy and celebration, and of worshipping Jesus as the King of kings, and yet of course it leads us into the events of Holy Week, the memory of sorrow and suffering, and finally death on a cross. We cannot think of one without the other, and any talk of the majesty of Jesus must be understood in the light of all that followed. The one we serve came to serve others. The Lord of life endured the darkness of death. The way to the throne involved the costly path of sacrifice. It is easy enough to sing Christ's praises and acknowledge him as Lord; it is a different matter to take up our cross and follow him. Yet that is the homage he asks of us and the challenge this day brings. As we offer today our glad hosannas let us ask ourselves if we are ready also to offer ourselves in his service.

Hymn *Listen to the shouts of praises*
Make way

Prayer

Lord Jesus Christ,
you had no interest in serving yourself,
only in serving others;
you did not desire your own glory,
only the glory of him who sent you;
and because of that God has highly exalted you,
giving you the name that is above every name.
Teach us today the true nature
of kingship, service and authority,

and so help us to honour you as you desire,
through loving God with heart, mind and soul,
and loving our neighbour as ourselves.
So may we build your kingdom,
until you return in glory
and gather all things to yourself.
Amen.

Slides and music

Trumpet Voluntary Clarke, during which Psalm 24:7-10 is read

Meditation of a Zealot

The Messiah – not coming?
Don't make me laugh!
He's coming, all right,
and it won't be much longer, you take it from me,
any day now, I shouldn't be surprised.
How do I know?
Well, it's obvious, isn't it?
Just look around you at the world we're living in –
the state of our society,
the corruption,
greed,
self-interest;
so much contrary to God's will –
do you really think he's going to sit back
and let that carry on for ever?
I can't see it, somehow.
No, he may be taking his time,
and the delay may be hard to understand,
but sooner rather than later
the day of the Lord will be here,
and what a day it will be,
what a moment for us all!
At last we'll be free,
a light rather than laughing stock to the nations,
a sovereign people instead of subject state,
for surely when he *does* come
the call to arms won't be far behind,
the sound of trumpets summoning us into battle
and onwards to victory.

That's what God's promised us, isn't it? –
a new kingdom,
a fresh start,
deliverance from slavery –
and I can hardly wait for it to begin.
Just imagine the scene if you can,
Jesus and Pilate head to head,
Roman governor versus King of the Jews –
that should be worth watching!
I could almost feel sorry for Pilate if I didn't hate him so much,
for he won't know what's hit him,
the might of his army powerless against the Lord's hand.
What will he do?
Oh, no doubt he'll wriggle and squirm a bit,
even wash his hands of all responsibility,
pretending it was all in the line of duty,
but there'll be no escape,
no way of avoiding final judgement,
for, remember, it's God's anointed we're talking about here,
the one who will come to establish justice and righteousness,
to drive out evil,
and finally, when the enemy is defeated, to bring us peace.
I know it's not been easy this time of waiting,
hoping against hope for some sign of the Messiah,
but God has promised that deliverance will come,
and what he says we know he will do.
So don't tell me he's not coming.
It's just a matter of time, nothing more,
the dawn of his kingdom round the corner,
here before you know it.
I only hope I'm still around when it arrives, able to see it for myself,
for it will have been worth waiting for, no doubt about that –
quite simply, out of this world!

Silence

Hymn *Ride on! ride on in majesty!*
Majesty, worship his majesty

Slides and music

Berceuse Godard, during which Luke 19:29-40 is read

Meditation of one of the owners of the colt ridden by Jesus

Hello, I thought, what's going on here?
And you can hardly blame me,
for there I was, minding my own business,
when suddenly these fellows I've never clapped eyes on
appeared from nowhere
and, cool as you like, started to make off with our donkey!
In broad daylight, too, that's what I couldn't get over –
bold as brass,
without so much as a by-your-leave!
Well, you can imagine my surprise, can't you?
Hardly the kind of goings-on you expect in a quiet village like ours.
So I asked them straight, 'What's your game?'
And that's when they spoke those special words:
'The Lord needs it.'
Not the fullest of explanations, admittedly,
but it was all I needed,
for straightaway it all came flooding back –
that day when Jesus came by
and for a wonderful few moments I met him face to face.
No, you won't have heard about it,
for it wasn't the sort of encounter to hit the headlines –
no stunning healing or unforgettable miracle needed in my case,
but he touched my life as surely and wonderfully as any,
offering a new direction,
a fresh start from which I've never looked back.
Quite simply, he changed my life,
and though I'm not the sort to shout it from the rooftops
I wanted to respond nonetheless,
to show Jesus how much he meant to me,
how much I valued what he'd done.
This was it,
the chance I'd been waiting for,
my opportunity to give something back at last.
Hardly earth-shattering stuff, I grant you –
the loan of a donkey –
but that didn't matter;
the fact was that Jesus had need of me –
it was all I needed to know.
He arrived soon after, and I followed him to Jerusalem,
where the crowds were waiting to greet him,
wild with excitement,

shouting their praises,
throwing down their cloaks in welcome –
and, small though it had been, I knew I'd done my bit
to make that great day possible.
Never forget that, whoever you are,
however little you think you have to offer,
for some day, some time, your moment will come –
a day when your contribution to his kingdom
will be requested in those lovely words:
'The Lord needs it.'

Silence

Slides and music

Osanna in excelsis J. S. Bach, during which Matthew 21:1-11 is read

Meditation of Simon the Zealot

You should have heard them!
What a noise!
What a sight!
What a welcome!
I'm telling you, I've never seen the like,
not in all my born days,
and there's been a few of those.
We've had kings here,
governors,
would-be messiahs,
and they've all had their moments,
their fans out in force to greet them,
but nothing like this,
nowhere near it!
They came in their thousands,
waiting to meet him,
the news of his coming having raced before him.
And it wasn't just his followers,
it was everyone,
men, women and children plucking branches from the trees,
tearing off their cloaks,
carpeting the road before him,
their voices hoarse with shouting.
'Hosanna!' they cried.
'Blessed is he who comes in the name of the Lord!'

It was treason, of course,
and probably heresy too,
but no one cared –
devil take the consequences, this was a time for rejoicing,
and rejoice we did.
Yet if that was unusual –
the abandonment,
the jubilation –
there were stranger things to follow,
for just a few days later,
less than a week in fact,
the scene was so very different.
The same people by and large,
once more part of a crowd,
but this time not love but hatred in their faces,
not welcome but rejection,
their waving hands suddenly shaking fists,
their 'Hosanna to the Son of David'
all at once 'We have no king but Caesar'.
I wouldn't have believed it possible if I hadn't seen it for myself,
but the sad fact is I not only saw it,
in my own way I was part of the whole sorry business,
for when the crisis came I was found wanting,
concerned only to save my skin
with no thought as to his.
It was a chilling lesson,
and one that I, like so many others, learned the hard way –
the lesson that it's easy to call someone king,
much harder to actually serve them.

Silence

Prayer

Lord Jesus Christ,
servant of all,
friend of all,
saviour of all,
ruler of all,
receive our worship.
To you be glory and honour,
praise and thanksgiving,
this day and for evermore.
Amen.

Hymn *All glory, laud and honour*
Meekness and majesty

Blessing

Music *Rex Tremendae (Requiem)* Mozart

Maundy Thursday

Suggested visual material	Jesus of Nazareth 5 and 6 Oberammergau 1990 The Life of Christ III and IV He Carries our Cross Bread and Wine Man of the Cross
Suggested music	Rather than use separate pieces of music, I have suggested here the use of one continuous piece, excerpts faded in and out as appropriate.
Music	*Adagio (Symphony No. 2 in E minor)* Rachmaninov (excerpt – total length 14:59)
Introduction	'The Lord Jesus Christ on the night when he was betrayed took a loaf of bread, and when he had given thanks, he broke it and said, "This is my body that is for you. Do this in remembrance of me." In the same way he took the cup also, after supper, saying, "This cup is the new covenant in my blood. Do this, as often as you drink it, in remembrance of me."' (1 Corinthians 11:23b-25). These are words which always have the power to move and inspire us, no matter how many times we hear them. But tonight, of all nights, they have a special poignancy, for we are here to recall that night long ago when the words were first spoken and the chain of events to which they point was to be set into motion. Events which were to reveal evil at its worst and good at its best; hatred at its most ugly and love at its most beautiful. We reflect on those events this evening through focusing on four of those most intimately involved in them – Philip, Judas Iscariot, a soldier from the cohort sent to arrest Jesus, and Annas the high priest. But above all we focus on Jesus – this man who aroused such passion for and against him, such fierce devotion yet such bitter rejection; a man whose unique character demanded a response from all he met, just as it goes on demanding a response from us today.

Hymn *Now, Jesus, we obey your last and kindest word*
Lord Jesus Christ, you have come to us

Prayer

Lord Jesus Christ,
we are here at your invitation –
here to share, as so many have shared before us,
in your supper,
this simple act which you commanded us to do
in remembrance of you.
We come, then, to remember –
to remind ourselves of all you suffered
to set us free,
to recall the extent of your love
and the enormity of your sacrifice.
But we come also to celebrate –
to rejoice in all you have done for us
through your death,
and to thank you for all you go on doing for us
through what you achieved there on the cross.
Lord Jesus Christ,
you broke bread,
you poured wine,
your body broken,
your blood shed for us.
Help us, as we eat and drink together,
to receive you more completely into our hearts,
to welcome you more fully into our lives,
and so to represent you more truly
as your body here on earth,
until that day when we are wholly one with you,
and you are all in all.
Amen.

Slides and music

Adagio (Symphony No. 2 in E minor) Rachmaninov (excerpt)
during which Mark 14:17-25 is read

Meditation of Philip

He couldn't mean me, surely? –
that's what I kept telling myself –
one of the others perhaps, but not me.

I would stay true, if nobody else did,
dependable to the last,
someone he could stake his life on if he needed to.
Yet could he?
Deep down, despite my protestations, I wondered,
for, to tell the truth, I was scared out of my wits,
dreading what the future might hold for us.
It was suddenly all too real,
the prospect of suffering and death,
those warnings Jesus had given
no longer simply words we could push aside,
but fact staring us in the face.
His enemies were gathering for the kill,
greedily waiting their moment,
and it was only a matter of time
before they came for the rest of us.
We'd kept on smiling until then,
putting a brave face on things as best we could,
if not for his sake then our own.
But suddenly there could be no more running away,
for in that stark sentence he spelt out the awful truth:
'One of you will betray me.'
We protested, of course, vehement in our denials,
yet one by one we looked away, unable to meet his gaze.
It *wasn't* me, I'm glad to say,
but, of course, you'll know that by now, won't you?
It was Judas who finally couldn't take it,
Judas whose name will go down in history
as the one who betrayed Jesus.
Yet somehow that doesn't help,
for the truth is this:
when the moment came we were all found wanting,
all more concerned for our own safety than his.
Maybe we didn't betray him,
but don't think we're feeling smug about it,
still less like twisting the knife in Judas,
for that moment – there in the upper room –
made us all take a long hard look at ourselves,
and we didn't much like what we saw.

Silence

Slides and music

Adagio (Symphony No. 2 in E minor) Rachmaninov (excerpt)
during which John 13:21-30 is read

Meditation of Judas

'Do what you have to do,' he told me.
And I realised then, as he looked at me,
  from the expression in his eyes,
  that he knew full well what I'd been up to,
  and understood precisely what I had planned for later that evening.
Call me a fool, but I thought until then I'd covered my tracks,
  played the part of doting disciple to a tee.
And I was right to a point,
  for my fellow apostles fell for it hook, line and sinker.
You should have seen their faces
  when Jesus suddenly turned during supper
  and solemnly announced that one of us would betray him.
'Who is it, Lord?' they gasped. 'Surely not I?'
But they actually believed it might be –
  as much one of them as me.
Not Jesus though –
  I realised the moment he looked at me
  that there was no pulling the wool over *his* eyes.
He saw through the charade,
  behind the lamb to the wolf,
  beneath the dove to the serpent,
  and suddenly I was ashamed,
  sickened by what I was doing,
  disgusted at what I'd become.
I should have stopped it there and then,
  confessed everything before them all and begged for mercy.
But I didn't.
I was too proud,
  afraid of losing face,
  terrified of what Caiaphas might do to me
  if I failed to deliver the goods.
So I slithered out of the room,
  leaving the rest of them wide-eyed in disbelief.
It still wasn't too late, even then –
  I could have called a halt to the whole business,
  and I only wish I had.

But I didn't –
I led the soldiers into the garden,
and greeted Jesus with a kiss –
the last revolting act of a repulsive evening.
It was bad enough betraying a friend,
but what made it worse
was that we'd eaten together such a short time before.
He'd washed my feet,
shared bread and wine,
kept faith with me to the very last, despite everything.
If he'd cursed me,
accused me,
rebuked me,
it would have made it easier.
If he'd only shown some sign of resentment,
maybe then I could have lived with myself,
knowing he wasn't so perfect after all.
But there was none of that.
A hint of sorrow, perhaps,
but apart from that, only love,
compassion, forgiveness.
He knew what was happening, yet it made no difference.
He knew I was leading him to his death,
and he carried on regardless.
Why?
You tell me!
I only hope he had more idea what he was doing than I had.

Silence

Celebration of the Eucharist

Slides and music

Adagio (Symphony No. 2 in E minor) Rachmaninov (excerpt)
during which John 18:1-14 is read

Meditation of the Temple policeman

Why didn't he escape while he had the chance? –
that's what I can't work out.
He had only to melt away into the shadows,
slip quietly off into the darkness,

and we'd have missed him for sure,
our quarry once again slipping through our fingers.
Right fools we'd have looked then!
But, luckily for us, it didn't work out that way.
Don't ask me why, for I still can't make sense of it,
but for some reason he actually came looking for us,
determined, apparently, to give himself up.
Was he fed up, perhaps, with the constant harrying,
the knowledge that we were always there,
plotting behind his back,
waiting for the chance to bring him down.
Some have said so,
yet he'd never appeared troubled before,
our attentions, seemingly, of no importance to him.
Whatever it was, though, the fact is *he* took the initiative,
and we were taken aback,
such assurance the last thing we'd expected.
You should have seen us,
enough men and weapons to bring down an army,
and there he was surrendering without a murmur,
even rebuking that hot-headed disciple of his
for taking a swipe at Malchus.
It was astonishing,
yet that's how it continued –
no argument,
no resistance,
no attempt to defend himself –
not even when he stood before Pilate,
his life on the line.
He submitted willingly,
almost eagerly,
like a lamb led to the slaughter.
Well, we achieved what we were sent to do.
We got our man where we wanted him,
nailed for all to see on a cross.
Yet somehow it doesn't feel right,
the whole business leaving a strange taste in the mouth,
for the truth of the matter is this:
we didn't take his life from him as we'd planned –
he gave it to us!

Silence

Slides and music

Adagio (Symphony No. 2 in E minor) Rachmaninov (excerpt)
during which John 18:19-24 is read

Meditation of Annas

Angry? You bet I was!
Wouldn't you have been?
It beggared belief the things this man had said and done –
violating the sabbath,
flouting the scripture,
contradicting our teaching,
presuming even to forgive sins –
who did he think he was, the Son of God or something?
I was seething,
barely able to restrain myself as he stood before me,
so when one of my men lashed out
and struck him across the face,
let's put it this way, I made no attempt to intervene.
It wouldn't have been so bad had he been a priest or a rabbi –
at least then he'd have had some claim to authority,
some grounds perhaps to speak out.
But he wasn't any of those, was he? –
just some self-styled teacher from Galilee
without even the first idea about the finer points of the law.
Yet was he sorry when they dragged him in?
Was there any sign of remorse,
even a hint of regret?
Not a bit of it!
Blatant defiance, more like,
a total disregard for his spiritual betters.
I'll give him one thing, though –
he made no attempt to duck the issue as some might have done,
no cowering behind half-truths or lame excuses.
We'd been prepared for that,
even hauled in some false witnesses just in case,
but it was clear they wouldn't be needed,
this man happy, apparently, to condemn himself
out of his own mouth.
That's the one thing I can't understand –
he made it easy for us,
almost too easy,

as though he wanted it all to happen,
as though he welcomed the prospect of death.
It wasn't just the trial that set me thinking, but before that:
why, for example, he came to Jerusalem in the first place –
he must have known the knives were out for him;
and why he waited there in the garden
after Judas slipped away into the darkness –
did he really have no idea we'd set him up?
Perhaps he was just teasing us,
believing God would deliver him at the last?
Or did he expect the mob to rise up in rebellion,
to take us by storm and set him free?
Well, if he did, he showed no sign of it.
It's a mystery to me, I have to confess,
and there are times when I catch myself thinking
we were the ones set up that night,
not *him* –
that for all *our* scheming *he* was the one
who finally called the tune.
I'm wrong of course,
I must be,
for where did it get him? –
off to Caiaphas,
off to Herod,
off to Pilate,
off finally to the cross and that ghastly, grisly end.
Not even Jesus could have wanted that, could he?
Surely not!

Silence

Prayer
Lord Jesus Christ,
we have eaten the bread and drunk from the cup,
and so once more proclaimed your death.
Now let us go back to the world
and proclaim your death there,
through the people we are
and the lives we live.
May we make known your love,
make real your compassion,

make clear your grace,
and so make nearer your kingdom,
until you come.
Amen.

Hymn *Love is his word, love is his way*
Come, let us sing of a wonderful love

Blessing

Music *Adagio (Symphony No. 2 in E minor)*
Rachmaninov (excerpt)

Good Friday

Suggested visual material
Jesus of Nazareth 5 and 6
Oberammergau 1990
The Life of Christ III
He Carries Our Cross

Music
He was despised (Messiah) Handel

Introduction
'Were you there when they crucified my Lord?' So asks that lovely and powerful hymn so often sung on or around Good Friday. The answer of course is that we weren't. But in the pages of Scripture we can read the testimony of those who *were* – those who experienced first-hand the grief, the horror, the pain, and the anguish of watching Jesus nailed to the cross. Today we listen again to their testimony, and we seek to get behind their words through asking what else each might have said to us about that day given the opportunity. We share in music, slides, readings and meditations, so that as far as possible, in imagination if not in the flesh, we can be there, confronted by the Christ who died for all; who died for us.

Hymn *Lord of the cross of shame*
There is a green hill far away

Prayer

Living God,
in so many ways this is the blackest of days
recalling the darkest of moments –
a day on which hearts were broken
and faith tested to the limit,
a day of appalling suffering and agonising death,
a day when all hell was let loose
and love seemed overwhelmed.
Yet we can call this day 'Good Friday',
for in all of that horror you were there.

In the despair, in the pain,
in the humiliation, in the sorrow,
you were supremely at work,
demonstrating the immensity of your love.
Living God,
as we recall those terrible yet wonderful events,
give us new insight into what you did that day,
for us and for all.

Slides and music

Clair de lune Debussy, during which Matthew 27:15-26 is read

Meditation of Pilate's wife

I told him not to get involved.
'Leave it alone,' I said,
'Stay out of it.
After all, you're the governor,
you're the one in charge.
Let the Jews sort it out,
send him off to Herod,
get someone else to do your dirty work for a change.
It's not your problem!'
So what did he do?
Made a right botch of things, that's what!
Oh, he tried all right, I'm not denying that;
he wanted to wash his hands of Jesus as much as I did,
more if anything.
I've never seen him so agitated,
so uncertain what to do.
And to be fair he took my advice, to a point;
sent the man off to Herod, just as I suggested.
But he let him send Jesus back, that's what I can't understand –
he let that cunning old devil off the hook
and left himself in the lurch.
Honestly, men!
After that it was downhill all the way.
'You decide,' he told the crowd,
'Barabbas, or Jesus?
It's up to you?'
Brilliant!
They could all see what he was angling for,
and they were damned if he was going to get it.

'Give us Barabbas!' they shouted,
 and you could almost hear the chuckle;
 they could scarcely keep the smirk off their faces.
So there he was,
 nowhere else to turn,
 no one else to turn to,
 the decision his and his alone.
Yet even then all wasn't lost;
 he should have stood up to the mob,
 listened to his conscience –
 not that he ever has before, mind you.
But when they suggested his loyalty might be suspect,
 his job on the line,
 that settled it.
Now look at him.
I thought *my* nerves were bad,
 but his – they're shot right through.
He just can't forget the man,
 night or day,
 never a moment's peace.
He's tormented by shame,
 riddled with guilt.
Well, I tried to warn him;
 I couldn't do more.
He made his decision, and now he has to live with it.
But I can't help wondering sometimes,
 when I look into his eyes,
 when I catch that haunted, hunted expression deep within,
 just who passed judgement on whom that day.
Was it Pontius who condemned Jesus?
Or was he the one condemned?

Slides and music

And with his stripes (Messiah) Handel, during which John 19:1-6a is read

Meditation of Nicodemus

His back was cut to ribbons,
 a criss-cross of bloodied weals,
 the skin hanging in tatters where the whip had torn away the flesh.
Yet still he said nothing –
 no cry for mercy,
 no howl of protest,

no shout of abuse –
nothing!
Apart from the grunts of pain,
the involuntary gasps,
he was silent.
And we were all amazed.
We'd seen hardened killers grovel under the lash,
prize-fighters cry like babies,
but not Jesus.
I have to admit it, I thought he'd crack, for all my admiration of the man;
I never imagined he could take such punishment.
A few strokes, perhaps,
a token resistance,
but then they'd break him and he'd say what they wanted him to,
admit he'd been wrong.
But it never came,
never happened,
never even looked like happening;
and suddenly I recalled the words of the prophet Isaiah,
that great vision of God's chosen servant
all at once imbued with new meaning –
'Like a lamb led to the slaughter
and like a sheep silent before its shearers,
so he did not open his mouth.
He was wounded for our transgressions,
crushed for our iniquities,
upon him was the punishment that made us whole,
and by his stripes we are healed.'
It was like a flash from heaven,
a ray of sunshine in a dark and dismal wilderness,
for I realised that there, in the face of such appalling suffering and evil,
there in the wretchedness of sorrow and death,
God was at work,
bringing health,
wholeness,
love,
life.
Did Jesus see it like that?
Was that the secret which gave him strength?
We'll never know.
But I'll tell you one thing:
it changed my life, seeing him suffer like that.

It made me realise that I had to respond,
had to follow him;
there was no other way.
For I knew it should have been me standing there enduring that agony;
it should have been you,
Caiaphas,
Pilate,
anyone –
anyone other than Jesus.
He poured himself out to death,
cut off from the land of the living,
and somehow, in a way I don't fully understand,
but a way I shall never, never forget,
he did it for us!

Hymn *O sacred head sore wounded*

Slides and music

Lacrimosa (Requiem) Mozart, during which Luke 23:32-38 is read

Meditation of Peter

He was bleeding,
my friend Jesus,
skewered to that cross,
like a piece of meat,
great drops of blood trickling slowly to the ground,
from his head,
from his hands,
from his feet.
I watched, stricken with horror,
numbed with grief,
as the life seeped away.
And I asked myself tearfully,
angrily,
why?
Why had God let it happen?
Why didn't he step in and do something?
What was he thinking of?
It seemed criminal,
a stupid, senseless waste to let such a wonderful man die –
let alone to die like that!

And for a moment my faith was shattered,
in myself,
in God,
in everything.
But then I remembered his words,
just the night before when we had broken bread together:
'This is my blood, shed for you and for many, for the forgiveness of sins.'
And even as I remembered, so that other time came back,
there by the Sea of Galilee after he had fed the multitude,
the crowd pressing round him asking for more:
'Whoever comes to me will never be hungry,
whoever believes in me will never be thirsty;
my flesh is true food and my blood is true drink.'
They had been a mystery to me until then, those words,
hard to stomach, if you'll pardon the pun.
But suddenly, there beneath that cross, I began to understand,
just a little,
only the merest fraction,
yet enough to help me realise it wasn't all in vain;
that somehow Jesus was hanging there for me,
for you,
for everyone.
I still ask why, mind you, and I think I always will,
for I'll never get that picture out of my mind;
that picture of Jesus broken on the cross.
Why that way, God, and not another?
Why not something less brutal,
less awful,
less messy?
Yet the strange thing is *he* never asked why,
not once in all the days I knew him.
Oh, he'd have liked there to be another way, of course;
he didn't want to die any more than the next man.
But he offered his life,
freely,
willingly,
lovingly,
in the conviction that, through his dying, we might truly live.

Slides and music

Behold the lamb of God (Messiah) Handel
during which Mark 15:22-26, 33-34 is read

Meditation of John

He was groaning,
a sound like I'd never heard before,
a sound I never want to hear again –
awful,
stomach-churning,
indescribable –
the sound of unimaginable pain,
of overwhelming sorrow,
of utter isolation.
And I could watch it no longer.
I thought I was ready for it,
prepared for the worst,
for I knew he had to die.
But I wasn't ready,
not for this;
I never realised people could suffer so much,
that anything could be quite so terrible.
But I know now,
and I'm telling you straight,
I'd have felt sorry for anyone facing that –
a robber,
a mugger,
even a murderer!
My heart would still have bled for them.
But to see Jesus there,
a man of such gentleness and compassion,
a man who had always loved and never hated,
a man who had brought healing to the sick
and wholeness to the broken,
it all but finished me.
What had he done to deserve this?
What crime had he committed?
What was it about him that aroused such passion,
such devotion,
yet such loathing?
I prayed that God would finish it,
put him out of his misery,
but still the torment continued,
still they mocked him, delighting in his pain.
I knew he was suffering, but even then didn't realise how much,
not until he lifted his head and I saw the despair in his eyes,

not until he spoke and I heard the wretchedness in his voice:
'My God, my God, why have you forsaken me?'
Then I realised,
and my blood ran cold.
He felt alone,
totally alone,
abandoned by everyone he'd loved and trusted,
even by God himself.
He could cope with the rest –
he'd even expected it –
but God?
It was the final torture,
the ultimate agony,
a pain beyond words.
He was groaning, a sound like I'd never heard before,
a sound which suddenly I understood,
and a sound I could listen to no longer.

Hymn *His hands were pierced*
When I survey the wondrous cross

Slides and music

Behold, and see (Messiah) Handel, during which John 19:25, 28-30 is read

Meditation of Mary, wife of Clopas

He was silent,
quite still,
his body limp and lifeless,
like a rag doll,
like a broken puppet.
And I thanked God that at last it was over,
his ordeal finally ended.
But it wasn't,
not quite.
He moved again,
just the faintest twitch,
the last flickering ember of life,
but enough to prolong our hopes,
enough to prolong his pain.
He was still breathing,
still suffering.

We watched wretchedly, torn by conflicting desires –
  the longing to see him come down and prove his enemies wrong;
  the longing to see him find peace in the cold embrace of death.
But suddenly his eyes were open,
  wide,
  bright,
  triumphant;
  the lips were moving,
  eager,
  excited,
  exultant;
  and his voice rang out:
  'It is finished!'
An acknowledgement of defeat, some said afterwards,
  a last despairing cry of sorrow.
But it wasn't,
  not for those who heard it,
  not for those with ears to hear.
It was altogether different –
  like sunshine after storm,
  like rain after drought,
  like laughter after tears –
  gloriously unexpected,
  wonderfully surprising.
He had stooped and conquered,
  staked all and won.
Defeat was victory,
  darkness was light,
  death was life.
I didn't see it then, mind you,
  I can't pretend that.
It was just a glimpse at the time,
  a glimmer barely understood.
But what I did see, with sudden staggering clarity,
  was that until that moment,
  until that last victorious shout,
  he had lived with the awful burden of holding the world's fate in his own
  and wondering whether he could see it through.
At last it was done –
  he had honoured his calling,
  fulfilled his mission,
  walked the way of the cross.

It was finished,
and with a song in his heart and joy in his eyes
he bowed his head and surrendered his spirit.

Slides and music

Surely (Messiah) Handel

Meditation of Mary Magdalene

It was over,
finished –
thirty-three years of life,
three years of ministry,
seven days of turmoil,
six hours of agony,
finally ended –
and I couldn't believe it.
Yes, I know that sounds daft, having stood there and watched him die,
having seen them drive the nails into his hands,
having watched the spear thrust in his side,
having witnessed his dying breath.
What else did I expect, you may ask?
What other outcome could there possibly have been?
And I understand all that, for I knew he was dying, of course I did.
Yet when it finally happened,
when the end came,
I was numb,
unable to take it in,
paralysed with grief.
It just didn't seem possible that this man Jesus,
whom we'd known and loved,
whom we'd trusted and followed,
who had been the very centre of our lives,
could have been taken from us,
snuffed out,
never to be seen again.
It wasn't that he hadn't prepared us,
you could never accuse him of that –
he'd spoken of death until we were sick and tired of hearing it.
And we honestly thought we were ready,
that we'd taken it all in,
come to terms with the inevitable,
steeled ourselves to face the worst.

But we hadn't,
not when it came to the wire.
The theory was one thing,
the reality something else.
I realised as we stood there,
the tears rolling down our faces,
our hearts torn in two,
that we'd always expected him in the final chapter to come up smiling,
put one over on those wretched Pharisees
and show them who was boss.
But of course it wasn't like that,
nothing like it at all.
It was over,
finished,
just like he'd said it would be,
and I couldn't get my head round it,
couldn't make sense of it whatever.
Yet there's one thing I've held on to since that awful moment;
one memory which has brought comfort even in the darkest of hours,
and that is those last words of his,
that cry he uttered with such dreadful yet confident finality:
'It is finished,' he shouted.
'It is finished!'
Words spoken not in sorrow,
not in anger,
nor in weary resignation,
but in a tone of sheer thanksgiving,
as though somehow even there,
especially there,
he had accomplished the very thing he came to do.

Prayer

Lord Jesus Christ,
living as we do in the light of Easter
we can lose sight sometimes
of the darkness of Good Friday.
But for those who were part of it
there could be no mistake,
no escaping the awfulness of seeing you
hanging there upon that Cross.

For them it was their darkest hour,
what seemed like the end of all their dreams,
and for a time their faith swung in the balance.
Yet even there, especially there, you were at work,
bringing your love to all.
Lord Jesus Christ,
teach us that even when life seems dark,
your light continues to shine.

Hymn *Beneath the cross of Jesus*

Blessing

Music *He was despised (Messiah)* Handel

Easter Day (1)

Suggested visual material
Jesus of Nazareth 6
The Life of Christ III and IV
Bread and Wine

Music
Vocalise in E minor Rachmaninov

Introduction
We are here to rejoice. We are here to give thanks. We are here to worship God, the giver of life. For today we remember that day which transformed the course of history and which across the years has transformed countless human lives. Easter Day – the day on which evil, sorrow and suffering, even death itself, were finally defeated; a day that makes every day and every moment a new beginning. Listen again to the words of Scripture, and listen also to reflections upon those words. Enter as best you can into the experience of those who witnessed the empty tomb and the risen Christ. For the message they heard, the Good News they celebrated, was not just for them but for us, and for all!

Hymn *Christ the Lord is risen today!*

Prayer

Lord Jesus Christ,
you appeared to different people
at different places, at different times –
to Mary in the garden,
to Cleopas and his companion
on the Emmaus road,
to the disciples in the upper room,
to your followers in Galilee.
Each had their own unique meeting with you,
and it was only when you met with them,
face to face,
that the truth dawned;
only then that they dared to believe
you were alive.

Lord Jesus Christ,
we cannot see you quite as they did,
but we too can meet with you
and experience the reality of your living presence.
Meet with us now, as we worship you,
as we gather in your name.

Slides and music

I know that my Redeemer liveth (Messiah) Handel
during which Mark 16:9-11 is read

Meditation of Mary Magdalene

They're not going to listen, I can tell you that now.
They've always been suspicious of me, right from the start,
wondering what Jesus was thinking of,
getting mixed up with someone like me.
I know what they'll say, you mark my words –
'Making it all up.'
'Wanting to be the centre of attention as usual.'
'A lovesick fool.'
Not that I can blame them;
it didn't do his cause any good, after all, when I came along.
A few tax-collectors those Pharisees could stomach,
but me, I really put the cat among the pigeons.
I know how the tongues wagged,
how easy it became to criticise.
Maybe I should have stayed away,
kept my distance,
but I loved him.
No, not in the sense they meant with their sly, dark innuendo,
but deeper,
with everything I am,
everything I've got,
in a way that I've never loved before.
Yet not even the disciples really trusted me, I know that.
They found it hard to accept,
hard to forgive what I'd been.
And I can understand that –
let's face it, I'm finding it hard to forgive them for running away,
failing him when he needed them most.
But what I hold on to is those words from the cross:
'Father, forgive them, for they do not know what they do.'

He understood we all fail him,
that we're all unworthy,
none of us perfect,
yet he forgave us and loved us despite that.
I thought I'd lost him,
the only one who ever truly accepted me,
and I was reconciled to struggling on alone,
no one to understand,
no one to offer their support.
But I was wrong, for he came to me.
There in the garden, overwhelmed by my grief,
he came to me, and hope was born again.
Not that I could believe it at first.
The voice was familiar,
the face,
the eyes,
but I told myself it couldn't be,
that it had to be the gardener,
anyone but Jesus.
And they'll do the same, I'm sure of it,
tell me I got it wrong,
that I'm overwrought,
ready to believe anything.
They won't listen, I can tell you that now,
but then I'm used to that, aren't I?
And it doesn't matter any more,
for he's accepted me
as he's accepted them,
as he accepts everyone who's ready to respond to his love
and receive his forgiveness.

Hymn *Led like a lamb to the slaughter*

Slides and music

Morning (Peer Gynt) Grieg, during which Luke 24:13-20, 25-31 is read

Meditation of Cleopas

So that's who it was!
I see it now, staring me in the face.
But how could we have not realised it before?
That's what I don't understand.

You see, we'd been to Jerusalem,
  watched with our own eyes what they did to him,
  even stood at the foot of the cross,
  yet we didn't recognise him when he walked beside us.
Why?
Was it sorrow that blinded us,
  our hearts too full of grief to glimpse the truth?
It's possible, for we were devastated, there's no denying that;
  we'd thought he was the one we longed for,
  coming to redeem our people,
  and it had been a terrible blow after arriving full of hope,
  anticipating his kingdom,
  to see him nailed to that cross,
  bruised and broken,
  the life seeping from his bleeding body.
We'd been so certain,
  so sure he was the Messiah,
  but we'd seen his death
  and were making our way back home,
  our dreams in tatters,
  our lives in ruins.
That could have clouded our eyes, unquestionably,
  for we had little time for anything or anyone.
He was the last person we expected to meet, I can tell you that.
Oh, I know he'd talked of rising again,
  returning from the grave –
  we were talking of it even as we walked –
  but we'd taken it all with a pinch of salt,
  and in our hearts we'd given him up,
  reluctantly making our way back to reality.
We never imagined for a moment we might see him;
  the thought simply never entered our heads.
So yes, perhaps that explains it,
  why for all that time the penny failed to drop.
Yet it was more than that,
  for it wasn't finally the face we recognised at all.
It went far deeper –
  the way he spoke,
  the way he acted,
  the way our hearts burned within us as we walked.
And above all the meal that we shared.
He took the bread,

and broke it,
and suddenly we realised, with a certainty nothing could shake,
that this was Jesus,
risen,
alive,
victorious.
Yet even as we saw it he disappeared,
vanishing before our eyes,
and we've never seen him since.
It's funny that, isn't it,
how we saw him most clearly when we couldn't see him at all,
how our eyes were opened when we weren't even looking –
and how we know he's with us now, even though he's departed from us!

Hymn *Jesus Christ is risen today*

Slides and music

Hallelujah Chorus (Messiah) Handel, during which John 20:19-20 is read

Meditation of Andrew

We've seen Jesus!
No, don't laugh,
we've seen him, I tell you!
We made the mistake of dismissing it ourselves,
scoffing when the women came racing back wild-eyed with excitement.
'Pull yourselves together!' we told them,
'For God's sake calm down!'
We couldn't believe he was alive,
refused to accept it could possibly be true.
And when they admitted they couldn't be certain,
that they'd only seen the empty tomb rather than Jesus himself,
then we looked for some simpler explanation,
an answer more in line with common sense.
Even when Mary returned, tears of joy in her eyes,
even when the two from Emmaus spoke of having seen him,
we wouldn't accept it, certain that we knew best.
It's understandable, I suppose;
I mean, you'd think twice, wouldn't you,
if you'd seen your best friend murdered,
sealed in the tomb,
only to be told he'd been spotted down the street?
And anyway, we didn't want to build our hopes up.

We were still reeling from the shock, the horror, the sorrow of it all.
Yet if I'm honest there's more to it than that,
for most of all our pride was hurt.
If he was alive, we reasoned, then why hadn't we seen him?
Why should Mary,
or those two disciples,
or anyone else come to that,
have seen him before we did?
We were his chosen disciples,
we the ones who'd given up everything to follow him,
we those who had taken all the risks –
so if he had risen surely we'd have known?
It's awful, I know, but that's the way we saw it
until he finally appeared to us.
We should have remembered, of course, what he'd said so often,
how the first will be last,
the least greatest;
but we still had much to learn
and were too full of ourselves by half.
Anyway, there we were,
huddled together in that upstairs room,
arguing about what it all meant,
when there he was,
standing among us,
arms outstretched in welcome.
Where he came from or where he went after I've no idea.
I only know that it was him –
Jesus –
and that he was alive,
wonderfully,
amazingly,
gloriously,
alive!

Slides and music

Kyrie ('Coronation' Mass) Mozart, during which John 20:24-25 is read

Meditation of Thomas

Would you believe it!
They're all at it now, the whole daft lot of them!
I never thought I'd see the day.

Not Peter, anyway – I thought he had more sense.
And James and John, hot-headed at times perhaps,
but they had their heads screwed on, or so I thought.
OK, maybe the others were a little suspect.
Simon for one.
To be honest, I felt like he'd believe anything sometimes.
And the rest, they had their moments too, to put it kindly.
But this? Jesus alive and kicking, dropping in on them for a quiet chat . . .
who are they trying to kid?
It really is beyond me.
I mean, they were the first to mock when the women came back
trembling and laughing like a bunch of mixed-up children.
We all agreed it was nothing more than hysteria, poor things.
So what's changed? What's got into them?
If you ask me it's this cursed waiting:
waiting for the sound of footsteps,
waiting for the knock on the door,
waiting for the moment when we know it's all up for us
just as it was for him.
That's enough to make anyone go off their trolley.
But even so you won't catch me rabbiting on about Jesus being alive –
I'll want more than a few fanciful visions before I start doing that.
Let me touch him perhaps,
see the scars,
put my hand in that spear-wound,
feel where they smashed those nails home,
and then, who knows, it might be different.
But be honest, what chance is there of that?
Do you believe it could happen?
I don't.

Hymn *Low in the grave he lay*

Slides and music

Gloria (Mass in C minor) Mozart, during which Luke 24:36-43 is read

Meditation of James

I thought I'd seen a ghost.
no joking, I really did.
Oh, I shouldn't have done, I realise that –
not after everything Jesus had said,
and certainly not after the reports we'd heard

from those who'd seen him –
but we were still struggling to take it in,
more troubled than happy at the news,
afraid something spooky was going on.
And when suddenly he appeared, popping up out of nowhere,
I was absolutely petrified.
Well, we all were, let's be honest,
though none of us would admit it publicly.
We nearly jumped out of our skins when we saw him,
and though we composed ourselves afterwards,
tried to look as though we'd been expecting him all along,
we couldn't fool Jesus.
He'd seen our faces,
taken in our reactions at a glance,
and in his eyes I caught both surprise and disappointment.
'Why are you frightened?' he asked us.
'Why do you doubt so much?
Look and see, is it me, or isn't it?'
Yet it wasn't as simple as that,
not even after we'd seen his hands,
touched his feet,
felt his side.
We knew it was him, but we still couldn't quite believe it
despite what our eyes were telling us.
It was too good to be true, I suppose.
We were afraid to trust ourselves,
afraid it might all be wishful thinking, seeing what we wanted to see.
We didn't want to raise our hopes only to have them dashed again,
so we simply stood and gawped.
Yet there could be no denying it,
not when he ate with us,
talked with us,
laughed with us.
It was almost like it had been before,
he and us together,
and we knew then that somehow,
in a way we couldn't quite understand,
he'd come back to us!
Yet it wasn't quite how it used to be –
there was something different,
something about him we couldn't quite put our finger on.
It was Jesus all right,

unquestionably the man we had loved and followed,
and he was there by our sides, flesh and blood as we are.
But we realised that though he'd come back to us
we would have to let him go,
have to part again.
There could be no return to what had gone before,
no turning the clock back and pretending nothing had happened.
It was the end of a chapter,
a chapter we had wanted to go on for ever.
Yet it was also the beginning of another,
the turning of a new page,
with no knowing where it might lead.

Prayer

Lord Jesus Christ,
we thank you that you meet us day by day,
just as you met your disciples
in the days following your resurrection.
We thank you that your victory of good over evil,
of love over hate, of life over death
continues to make such a difference to our lives,
just as it did to theirs.
We thank you that for us too
you turn weakness into strength,
fear into confidence, and doubt into faith.
And we praise you that for each of us
there is always the assurance of a new beginning
when it seems like the end,
new hope where there seems only despair.

Hymn *Thine be the glory*

Blessing

Music *Vocalise in E minor* Rachmaninov

EASTER DAY (2)

Suggested visual material
Jesus of Nazareth 6
The Life of Christ III and IV
Bread and Wine

Music
Gloria in Excelsis Deo (Gloria) Vivaldi

Introduction
We are here in the season that gives meaning to all seasons, for without Easter there would be no gospel, no message, no Church, no faith. We could talk still, it's true, of the birth of Jesus, his life, his ministry and his death, but without the empty tomb and the risen Christ all this would finally be a tale of tragedy rather than triumph – a mirror of this world's ultimate impermanence rather than a window into the eternal purpose of God. No wonder today we celebrate! And what better way to do that than to think again of some of those whose lives were transformed by that first Easter, and, through reflecting on their experience, to meet the risen Christ afresh and open our lives to his renewing power.

Hymn *Jesus, stand among us*
Jesus lives! your terrors now

Prayer

Lord Jesus Christ,
it was not just you who was broken
that day you hung on a cross;
it was your disciples too,
their hearts broken just as surely,
their dreams and hopes snuffed out,
their faith cut from beneath them and laid to rest.
It was not just you who rose again
that day you emerged from the tomb;
it was your disciples too,
their hearts beating once more

with joyful anticipation,
their vision for the future reborn,
their faith rekindled,
bursting into unquenchable flame.
Come to us now where we are broken –
where love has died,
where hope has faded,
where faith has grown cold.
Reach out and touch us in body, mind and spirit,
and help us to walk in the newness of life
which you alone can bring.
In your name we ask it.
Amen.

Slides and music

I know that my redeemer liveth (Messiah) Handel
during which Matthew 28:1-10 is read

Meditation of Mary Magdalene

I'll never be able to say what it meant to me,
after the horror and the heartache,
the darkness and the despair,
to hear that wonderful, astonishing news –
Jesus, alive!
I'd lived in a daze until then,
unable to take in the horror of what I'd seen,
the anguish and the agony which he'd borne
with such quiet dignity and awesome courage.
He'd warned us to expect the worst,
and I suppose in our hearts we'd known what was coming
but we'd refused to accept it,
hoping against hope there might be some other way,
a path less costly, less awful for us all.
But as we walked that morning to the tomb,
all such thoughts were gone,
buried along with our Lord,
life dark, cold, empty,
bereft of meaning.
We were blind to everything in our grief,
scarcely aware even of the ground starting to shake
or light flooding around us,

but when we reached the stone, rolled away from the tomb,
we saw that all right,
and for a moment we just stood there gazing in confusion,
not knowing where to turn or what to say.
That's when it came, the news that took our breath away:
'He is not here.
He has been raised.
Come, see the place where he lay.'
We scarcely dared to look at first, afraid it might all be a dream,
but finally we found the courage,
and it was true,
he was gone! –
just the grave clothes left to show he'd been there.
You can imagine how we felt,
our hearts pounding with excitement;
but there was more to come,
things yet more wonderful,
for even as we ran to tell the news,
skipping with sheer delight,
we saw him ahead of us –
Jesus, the man we knew and loved,
arms outstretched in welcome,
waiting to greet us in his old familiar way.
He had risen, just as we'd been told,
death unable to hold him!
Only it wasn't just Jesus who rose that day,
it was all of us:
for there in the garden life began again,
life which we thought had died in us for ever –
hope reborn,
faith renewed,
love rekindled,
joy restored –
and we knew now these could never be destroyed –
the proof was there before us!

Silence

Slides and music

Gloria (Coronation Mass) Mozart, during which Luke 24:36-43 is read

Meditation of Peter

He was back!
Back in the land of the living,
  just when we'd given up hope!
Three days it had been,
  three days of dark despair as slowly the truth sank home –
  our Lord, laid in a tomb,
  dead and buried,
  never to walk this earth again.
We couldn't believe it at first,
  none of us,
  even though we'd seen it for ourselves.
We expected to wake up any moment to find it was all a dream,
  a dreadful mistake that had somehow taken us in.
But as the numbness passed, so the reality hit us,
  and the pain began in earnest.
It was an end to everything –
  our plans,
  our hopes,
  our dreams.
There was nothing left to live for,
  that's how we felt –
  we'd pinned our hopes on him,
  and he was gone.
Only he wasn't!
He was there,
  meeting Mary in the garden as her heart broke beside the tomb.
He was there,
  on the Emmaus road as two followers trudged slowly home,
  their world in tatters.
He was there,
  speaking to Thomas, breaking through his disbelief!
He was there,
  standing among us in the upper room!
He was back in the land of the living,
  and suddenly so were we –
  faith rekindled,
  hope renewed,
  joy reborn,
  life beginning again!

Silence

Hymn *Early on Sunday, Mary comes running*
Were you there when they crucified my Lord?

Slides and music

Why do the nations? (Messiah) Handel
during which Matthew 28:11-15 is read

Meditation of Caiaphas

They don't know when they're beaten, do they,
those followers of Jesus?
I really thought we'd put a stop to their nonsense, once and for all.
When we dragged that so-called Christ of theirs before Pilate,
when we saw them hammer the nails into his hands and feet,
when we watched as they sealed the tomb,
I was convinced that, at last, it was over,
the whole unfortunate business at an end.
After all, who wants a dead Messiah? –
what use could he be to anyone?
Preposterous, isn't it.
And yet, apparently not,
for I've received news this morning
that the body has vanished,
spirited away during the night.
God knows how it happened,
but it's the last thing we need right now –
you can just imagine the sort of stories
his followers will come up with,
even that he's been raised from the dead, I shouldn't wonder.
Absurd, I know,
but you'd be surprised what some people
are gullible enough to believe,
and if even a few are taken in who can say how many might follow?
So you'll understand, won't you, if we mould the truth a little? –
nothing patently false, of course;
just a little fine tuning here and there to fit the facts –
we've got it off to a fine art over the years.
Let's face it, it's obvious who's behind this charade –
I've no idea how they did it,
but somehow those wretched followers of his
must have got past the guards –
no doubt sleeping on the job, the good-for-nothing layabouts.

Anyway, that's the line we're taking,
and a few greased palms should ensure a united front,
enough to dispel any rumours.
There are a few points which trouble me, I must confess:
how they shifted that stone, for one thing,
and why they left behind his grave clothes, for another –
or was that all designed to add to the illusion?
Yet what I *really* can't understand is this:
why keep his name alive? –
what do they hope to prove? –
for they must know in their hearts that they're beaten,
the game over.
Even supposing some do fall for their trick,
it can't achieve anything,
for as the months pass without sight or sound of him
they're bound to question eventually,
and what a let-down it will all seem then.
You still have your doubts, even now?
Well, let me ask you this,
one question which should settle it for good:
twenty years from now,
a hundred,
a thousand,
who will talk about Jesus then? –
will anyone remember some obscure carpenter from Nazareth?
Need I say more?

Silence

Slides and music

Worthy is the lamb that was slain (Messiah) Handel
during which John 21:15-19 is read

Meditation of Peter

Three times he asked me,
three times the same simple yet searching question:
'Do you love me, Peter?'
And I was getting fed up with it,
not to say a little hurt.
After all, he should have known by then, surely?

I'd followed him for three years,
and I thought we'd become close –
he gave that impression, anyway.
The 'Rock', he'd called me,
the one on whom he'd build his Church –
an expression of trust, if ever there was one –
so how could he doubt me now,
let alone question my love?
But then, of course, I remembered that bold, brash promise of mine:
'Though all become deserters because of you,
I will never desert you' –
and suddenly I understood.
He'd known I would fail, even as I said it,
not only abandon but deny him,
and he knew too how sick I'd felt,
how wretched and ashamed
when the knowledge of my failure finally sunk home.
But there was no anger from him,
no recriminations,
no rebuke.
His concern was for me, not himself,
his sole desire to wipe the slate clean and start again,
and this was my chance to deal with the guilt,
to exorcise the demon once and for all.
Three times I'd denied him,
three times he put the question,
and at last I could put the record straight,
declare to him what I should have declared to others:
'Yes, Lord; you know that I love you.'
We couldn't change the past, we both knew that,
but with his help we could put it behind us and change the future,
and that's what he offered me that day;
a new beginning,
a fresh chapter,
life dawning for me as surely as it had dawned again for him.
I was restored,
cleansed,
forgiven,
the ghost finally laid to rest,
and I owed it all to him,
the man whom I abandoned so freely,
yet who refused to abandon me!

Silence

Celebration of the Eucharist

Prayer

Loving God,
 we praise you again for this season
 and the assurance it brings
 that nothing can ever finally overcome your love.
You confronted the forces of evil,
 allowing them to throw everything
 they could muster against you,
 and when they had done their worst
 you emerged victorious,
 no power able to hold you down.
Teach us always to hold on to that truth,
 and so to live each moment in the knowledge
 that, whatever we may face,
 your love will see us through.
In the name of the risen Christ we pray.
Amen.

Hymn *Low in the grave he lay*
This joyful Eastertide

Blessing

Music *Gloria in Excelsis Deo (Gloria)* Vivaldi

Ascension Day

Suggested visual material Jesus of Nazareth 6
In the Beginning
The Life of Christ IV

Music *Rex tremendae (Requiem)* Mozart

Introduction They had seen death, they had seen resurrection, and for the disciples of Jesus that sight of the risen Christ back among them must have seemed the most wonderful thing they could ever hope to witness. No wonder they asked the question that had been on each one's lips since his return: 'Lord, is this the time when you will restore the kingdom to Israel?' It had to be, surely? What more could be revealed than had been revealed to them already? The answer was just a few moments away, as suddenly Jesus was taken from them, and they were left struggling to come to terms with the unexpected once again. Whatever the precise event behind the language, one thing is clear – their picture of Christ had been far too small, their understanding of his purpose much too narrow. For he came not just to restore Israel but to redeem the world, not to rule on earth but to be enthroned in heaven. They had glimpsed the man but not the face of God beneath. They believed they saw the whole picture, when they saw but one piece of the jigsaw. Suddenly they had to think again, for Jesus was greater than they had begun to imagine. The same, I suspect, may be true for us all.

Hymn *The head that once was crowned with thorns*
Come and see the shining hope

Prayer

Lord Jesus Christ,
you are greater than we can ever imagine,
before all,
beyond all,
in all,
over all.
Forgive us for losing sight of your greatness,
for underestimating the breadth of your love
and the extent of your purpose,
for tying you down to the things of earth
rather than opening our hearts
to the kingdom of heaven.
Broaden our vision,
enlarge our understanding,
deepen our faith,
kindle our imagination,
that we may glimpse your glory,
and work more faithfully for your kingdom.
In your name we ask it.
Amen.

Slides and music

Dies irae (Requiem) Mozart, during which Mark 13:3-13 is read

Meditation of Andrew

It was a chilling picture he gave us,
so unlike those he usually painted,
so different from those we'd come to expect –
one which shattered all our illusions,
throwing everything we thought we'd understood into the balance.
No homely parables this time to bring the message home,
no comforting promises,
but a scenario which made us draw our breath in amazement –
stark,
shocking,
scary –
warnings of doom and disaster,
of trials and temptation,
of beatings and betrayal.

I don't know why,
but we'd never thought of the future in that way before,
never expected anything other than joy and blessings.
Not that we had a clear picture, mind you –
we were more interested in this world than the next –
but when the kingdom did come
and the sheep were separated from the goats,
well, we were pretty confident which side we'd be on.
Only, listening to Jesus, suddenly we weren't so sure after all.
His words wiped the smiles off our faces,
sent shivers down our spines,
for they brought home as never before the cost of discipleship,
the faith, commitment and perseverance needed
to see our journey through to the end.
We'd imagined, until then, it would be plain sailing,
a matter simply of plodding along until the race was run,
the sacrifices we might make now
more than compensated when the prizes were handed out.
But here was a different prospect altogether,
the possibility that our love might grow cold,
our faith be undermined,
our courage fail,
our horizons be clouded –
and the awful thing was we knew it could too easily come true.
We'd grown smug,
complacent,
too certain of our righteousness,
too blasé about our destiny;
but we realised then there could be no shortcuts,
no easy options –
the way is hard and the gate narrow,
and only a few will find it.
Yes, it was a chilling picture all right –
one that left us stunned and shaken –
yet I'm glad he painted it
for we needed to look again at the faith we professed,
to consider again the response we'd made,
and then to match our stride to his,
whatever it might take,
wherever it might lead.

Silence

Hymn *Alleluia! sing to Jesus*
Hail the day that sees him rise

Slides and music

On wings of song Mendelssohn, during which Acts 1:6-11 is read

Meditation of James

We stood there, speechless for a moment,
struck dumb by the enormity of it all,
for he was gone,
plucked away from before our very eyes
and, quite simply, we were lost for words,
stunned into silence.
It wasn't the first time, you see;
we'd lost him once already –
watched in horror as he was nailed to a cross, sealed in a tomb,
and we'd been devastated,
convinced we could never bounce back from such a blow.
We wouldn't have, either,
not by ourselves,
but suddenly he was back,
there in the garden,
there on the roadside,
there in the upper room –
our Lord, alive, risen, victorious,
death unable to hold him!
I just can't tell you how wonderful that was,
how our hearts skipped and our spirits soared
each time we saw him.
We felt certain nothing could ever again destroy our happiness,
for he had taken on the last enemy
and emerged triumphant!
Life, all at once, pulsated with promise,
no problem too great for us,
no challenge too daunting,
for, with Christ by our side, what had we to fear?
Yet suddenly, as we stood there that day gazing into heaven,
he was by our side no longer,
and for an awful moment
it seemed as though all our hopes had disappeared again,
vanishing with him like a bubble on the wind.

Only, of course, this time was different,
for we'd made time to listen,
paid heed to his warnings,
and we understood that, as he had departed,
so finally he would return.
You should see us now,
our faith, if anything, stronger today than it's ever been!
We've spoken more boldly and witnessed more powerfully
than I thought possible –
preaching the word,
healing the sick,
renewing the weak,
uplifting the broken-hearted,
carrying the good news of Jesus far and wide.
And I'll tell you why:
because his going that day
has somehow brought him closer than he's ever been before,
filling our whole being – body, mind and soul –
transforming our every thought and word and deed.
He's here,
he's there,
he's everywhere,
no person beyond his love,
no situation beyond his purpose,
for he has not simply risen,
he has ascended –
Jesus, the man who lived and died amongst us,
who shared our flesh and blood,
one with the Father,
Lord of lords and King of kings,
nothing in heaven or earth able to separate us
from the wonder of his love.
And sometimes when I think of all that means,
once more I'm struck dumb,
stunned into silence by the enormity of it all,
for it's wonderful, isn't it? –
almost too wonderful for words!

Silence

Slides and music

Come, Lord (Fountain of Life) Rizza
during which Revelation 21:1-4; 22:5 is read

Meditation of John

I had a dream last night,
a wonderful, astonishing dream –
so real,
so vivid,
that it will live with me for the rest of my days.
I caught a glimpse of God,
enthroned in majesty,
encircled by the great company of heaven,
and there at his right hand,
exalted,
lifted up in splendour,
our Lord Jesus Christ,
King of kings and Lord of lords!
It was wonderful,
breathtaking,
indescribable.
Yet I have to share it with you somehow –
clutching at metaphors,
searching for the right words,
but at least giving you some idea of what I saw.
Why? I hear you say.
What does it matter if it was only a dream?
And I take your point.
Yet I have this feeling, deep within,
no – more than just a feeling – this certainty,
that God was speaking to me through that dream;
speaking to *me*,
to *you*,
to everyone with ears to hear and a mind to listen.
He was telling us that in all the chaos of this humdrum world;
all the changes and chances of this uncertain life;
despite all the pain,
all the suffering,
all the evil,
all the sorrow,
everything that seems to fight against him,
God is there,
slowly but surely working out his purpose.
And one day,
in the fullness of time,

his kingdom will come
and his will shall be done.
Don't ask me when, for I can't tell you that.
But though we may not see it
and though we may not feel it,
I am assured that he will triumph.
Joy will take the place of sorrow.
Life will follow death.
Love will be victorious!

Silence

Prayer

Baby of Bethlehem, born in a stable,
we worship you.
Child of Nazareth, full of grace and truth,
we acknowledge you.
Man of Galilee, teacher, preacher, healer, redeemer,
we praise you.
Son of David,
coming in humility to claim your kingdom,
we greet you.
Suffering servant, bruised, beaten, broken,
we salute you.
Lord of the empty tomb, risen and triumphant,
we honour you.
King of kings, exalted by the side of the Father,
we adore you.
Jesus Christ, our Lord and Saviour,
receive the homage we offer,
to the glory of your name.
Amen.

Hymn *Hail, thou once despised Jesus*
Restore, O Lord, the honour of your name

Blessing

Music *Rex tremendae (Requiem)* Mozart

Pentecost

Suggested visual material

Visual resources for this service are not easy to find, but slides from the following may be useful:

In the Beginning
Jesus of Nazareth 3, 4 and 6
The Life of Christ IV
St Paul
The Story of Saint Paul

Music

Laudamus te (Mass in C minor) Mozart

Introduction

One moment confusion and the next certainty; one moment doubt and the next faith; one moment despair and the next hope; one moment fear and the next confidence. All of this goes some way to describing what happened on that extraordinary day of Pentecost recorded in Acts chapter 2. But exactly what was going on? And how did those people directly affected make sense of their experience? In this service today we look at some of those whose lives in contrasting ways were transformed by the gift of the Holy Spirit – the Spirit that is equally able to transform our lives in turn.

Hymn *Breathe on me, breath of God*

Prayer

Lord Jesus Christ,
you told the disciples
to expect the gift of the Holy Spirit,
yet when it came it took them by surprise,
bursting into their lives
in a way beyond all their expectations.
Suddenly life for them was transformed,
full of untold possibilities.
Lord Jesus Christ,
you tell us to expect the gift of the Spirit,
yet we too are taken by surprise.

You want to transform our lives
to open the door to new horizons,
but we close our hearts
or tie you down to our own expectations.
Lord Jesus,
as we remember today
that day of Pentecost long ago,
help us to open our lives
to the movement of your Spirit now.

Slides and music

Cum Sancto Spiritu (Gloria) Vivaldi, during which Acts 2:1-4 is read

Meditation of Peter

We shouldn't have been surprised,
not if we'd had any sense;
it was what we'd been told to expect,
what he'd promised us.
But we never imagined anything quite so extraordinary.
We were waiting, it's true,
gathered together as so often before,
but we'd been doing that for days
and our confidence had taken a hammering.
We were going through the motions, that's all,
telling each other he hadn't forgotten us,
talking of the future as though we still believed in it,
yet wondering in our hearts if there was anything to look forward to.
I mean, what could we hope to achieve when all was said and done.
What reason to think that we, a motley bunch if ever there was one,
should fare better than our master?
We wanted to carry on his work, don't get me wrong:
we wanted to tell people what had happened,
help them find faith for themselves,
but how could we even hope to begin?
So we kept the doors locked
and sang our hymns
and said our prayers
and hid our doubts.
Until suddenly it happened!
I can't properly describe it even now,
but it changed our lives.

It was as though a mighty wind blew away the cobwebs,
a refreshing breeze revived our flagging faith,
a breath of air stirred our spirits.
As though a tiny spark rekindled our confidence,
a tongue of fire set our hearts aflame,
a raging inferno swept our fears away.
As though life had begun again,
the world become a different place,
and each of us been born anew.
I know that doesn't make sense,
but it's the best I can do.
You'll have to experience it for yourself to understand.
And you can, just as we did.
Believe me, we never would have thought it possible,
despite all Jesus said to us.
We were lost,
lonely,
frightened,
hopelessly aware of our weaknesses,
searching for any strengths.
We never thought we'd change a soul,
let alone the world,
but that's because we had no idea how God could change us!

Slides and music

Slow movement from *Concerto for two violins*, J. S. Bach
during which Acts 4:32-37 is read

Meditation of Barnabas

It wasn't much of a gift;
at least I didn't think so.
In fact, I didn't feel I had a gift at all,
not like the rest of them with all their stunning signs and wonders.
I envied them sometimes,
so often in the limelight,
stealing all the headlines –
prophets,
teachers,
workers of miracles,
speakers of tongues.

They were the ones who drew the crowds,
the ones who people noticed,
and all I did was plod quietly along,
living the faith in my own simple way,
speaking and doing and caring and sharing
as I believed Christ would have me do.
And then they gave me this name –
Barnabas,
'Son of Encouragement.'
It was all so unexpected,
a complete surprise,
for what had I done to deserve any such honour.
But then they told me,
one by one,
that of all the gifts they valued,
mine was chief among them.
A generous gesture,
a word of praise,
an expression of trust,
an act of love –
not causing gasps,
not making heads turn;
yet these, they told me
(though I'd never dreamt it nor even realised they'd been done),
these had stirred their hearts and cheered their spirits
as signs and wonders could never do.
It doesn't seem much, does it –
encouraging people?
Not a gift you'll find in any of the textbooks,
nor one people will ever fight over.
Yet don't let that fool you as it did me –
don't waste time thirsting for those showy gifts you do not have –
for it's often when you're least aware of it,
through things you count unimportant,
that Jesus chooses to use you.
So if you are wondering, as I did, why you've been left out,
if you're feeling down,
or doubting your experience,
or waiting for the spirit and perplexed he hasn't come,
let me offer you some simple words of encouragement:
follow Jesus,
faithfully,

simply,
and maybe,
just maybe,
you'll find his spirit's been there all along.

Hymn *Come down, O love divine*

Slides and music

O death where is thy sting? (Messiah) Handel
during which Acts 6:8-10, 12-15 is read

Meditation of Stephen

I'm too young to die,
far, far too young!
There's still so much to live for,
so much I want to do,
so much I've barely started.
It's not that I'm afraid of death,
don't get me wrong.
It's just that I love life
and I don't want to let it go unless I have to.
I love the sound of birds singing in the trees,
the wind whispering through the grass,
children laughing in the street.
I love the sight of clouds scudding across the sky,
the sun setting across the ocean,
the trees laden with summer fruits.
I love the feel of water fresh upon my skin,
the smell of flowers dancing in the breeze,
the taste of food, steaming from the oven.
I love the joy of sharing with my family,
the pleasure of being among friends,
the warmth of Christian fellowship –
so much that is good which I just don't want to lose.
So why throw it away, I hear you ask me?
Why take a path that surely leads to death?
I've asked that too, believe me, countless times,
searching for another way,
an easier way that doesn't cost so much.
And yet although I wish there was,
I know deep down there isn't.

I could have steered a different course – no doubt that's true –
denied my faith or kept it under wraps.
I could have toned my message down or run away,
not trod on toes or taken risks.
Yet what if Christ had done the same, I ask you that –
put safety first and not caused such a stir?
What future then would we have had?
What hope, what joy, what faith to share?
But no, he gave his all,
despite the pain,
despite the fear,
despite the sorrow –
pursuing the way of love even to the cross.
That's why I'm here now,
jostled by the crowds,
dragged through the streets,
waiting for the stones to fly.
I don't want to die,
but neither did Jesus.
I'm too young to die,
but so was he.
I want to live
for I love life,
passionately,
deeply –
but the thing is I love Jesus even more,
just as he loved me.

Slides and music

Gratias (Mass in C minor) Mozart
during which John 1:43-46 and Acts 8:4-8 are read

Meditation of Philip

I have to tell you!
Forgive me if I'm intruding,
barging in where I'm not wanted,
but I have to tell you what Christ has done for me.
I'm not bragging, God forbid!
There's been no merit on my part,
nothing about me that's special or deserving of praise.

I'm just an ordinary, everyday person,
no different from anyone else,
but I've suddenly discovered what really matters in life,
what really counts.
I thought I knew already;
well, we all do, don't we?
A good job,
loving partner,
nice home,
children –
you know the sort of thing.
And don't think I'm knocking those,
for they can all be precious,
all offer their own fulfilment.
But when I heard about Jesus,
met him for myself,
suddenly I discovered there is something else,
something more important than any of those,
able to give a whole new perspective on them all,
and to answer my deepest needs.
I was set free from myself,
my guilt,
my sin,
my shame;
not suddenly becoming perfect
but finding forgiveness,
a new beginning,
a multitude of new beginnings.
I was set free from the endless quest for pleasure,
from the gods of greed and lust,
pride and envy;
learning there is more to life than the thirst for gain
or the pursuit of success.
I was set free from fear and worry,
despair and sorrow;
even in my darkest days certain joy will surely come.
And above all I've been freed from death,
knowing though this life shall end that I shall rise again!
So now do you see why I have to tell,
why I have to let you know?
I've found so much,
such hope,

such peace,
such happiness;
and I can't just sit on that as though it's mine and mine alone.
I have to pass it on,
share it out,
let you find it too;
so forgive me if I'm intruding,
but if you've got a moment,
please, please,
let me tell you!

Hymn *Spirit of the living God*

Slides and music

Adagio from *Clarinet Concerto* Mozart
during which 2 Timothy 1:1-7 and 1 Timothy 4:11-16 are read

Meditation of Timothy

I was only a boy,
a mere slip of a lad compared to most of them,
and I really wondered what use I could be.
My heart was willing,
positively bursting to get involved.
My faith was strong,
bubbling up like a mountain spring from deep within,
but I wondered whether anyone would accept me
and whether I had any right to expect them to.
They had more experience of life after all,
a store of wisdom accumulated over the years;
so why should they listen to someone half their age
just because he believed God had called him?
Yet though a few balked at the idea,
most had no objections.
They treated me with kindness,
friendship,
genuine respect;
and if occasionally I went too far,
carried away by youthful exuberance,
they responded patiently,
more than willing to make allowances.

None more so than Paul,
  my dear friend Paul.
How much I owe that man!
How much he changed my life!
Guiding me and helping me along the way of Christ.
And yet, though I've often tried to thank him,
  he's always shrugged it off,
  saying it's not him but Jesus I ought to thank.
Jesus who valued young and old,
  Jesus who welcomed little children,
  Jesus who's chosen me.
I've held on to that,
  day by day,
  year by year,
  and now suddenly it is I who am old,
  receiving from those who are young,
  I who have to recognise that God can work through all.
It's hard to accept that sometimes,
  even for me,
  until I look back,
  and remember those days long ago.
For I realise then, once again, that if Christ could use me
  he can use anyone!

Slides and music

Love's Theme from *Midnight Express*
during which 1 Corinthians 13:1-13 is read

Meditation of Paul

He taught me the meaning of love,
  what it really means to say, 'I love you'.
Slowly,
  gently,
  he taught me.
Not through words,
  nor through gestures,
  but through showing me love in action.
I thought I'd understood,
  that I loved as much as the next man, maybe more.
Not perhaps as a husband loves his wife, or a father his children –
  there's not been time for that, sadly –

but deeper,
beyond such natural ties –
my fellow apostles,
my family in Christ,
my fellow human beings.
And I did love in my own way, of course I did –
my only goal,
my single aim,
to help them,
serve them,
reach them.
And yet, despite all that, I sometimes wondered if I'd ever loved at all,
for deep down, in my heart of hearts, I knew it was all about me –
my preaching, *my* striving, *my* loving;
my efforts, *my* successes, *my* ambitions –
all finally for my own satisfaction
and even, I fear, my own glory as much as his.
It's human, I realise that, or so at least we tell ourselves,
but is that true?
Or does it have to be?
For when I look at Jesus,
all he did for me,
I see a different truth,
a different kind of love;
patient, kind, humble;
not serving self or seeking gain,
but putting others first.
A love that knows me as I am,
understands my faults,
yet still believes in me.
A love which, though I turn away, accepts me,
even dies for me!
That's what it means, this thing called love,
seeing the worst, believing the best,
asking nothing, and giving all.
I thought I'd understood, all those years ago,
but I hadn't, hardly at all.
I'm still learning even now,
still struggling to let go of self.
I can't do it alone,
I've come to realise that at last;
I need his help, his love flowing through me,

and I'll carry on praying for that,
striving for that,
until my dying day,
for I understand now that without love all else is nothing.

Prayer

Gracious God,
we thank you for those extraordinary moments
we occasionally experience
which change our lives,
giving us joy and fulfilment
we never imagined possible.
We thank you especially for the great gift
of your Holy Spirit –
an experience which transformed
the lives of the apostles,
which has changed the lives
of countless believers across the centuries,
and which has power to reshape our lives
here and now.
Open our hearts, our minds and our souls
to your living presence
so that we shall know your life-changing power
for ourselves.

Hymn *O Holy Spirit, breathe on me*
Awake, O Lord, as in the time of old

Blessing

Music *Valse Brilliante in E flat major* Chopin

Trinity Sunday

Suggested visual material

In the Beginning
Come, let us adore
Jesus of Nazareth 6
The Life of Christ IV

Music

En Trinitatis Speculum (Magnificat) Praetorius

Introduction

We are here today on Trinity Sunday, a day that perhaps captures the imagination less than any other in the Christian year, and to a point that is understandable, for rather than historical events this date in the calendar is concerned with an abstract doctrine that has perplexed theologians and ordinary believers alike across the centuries. Yet complex though the issues may be, we do well to reflect on them, for this should be a day that captures the imagination like no other, reminding us of the sheer breathtaking reality which we describe as God. We try to pin that reality down as best we can; to talk about our experience in terms of God the Father, the Son and the Holy Spirit, but we are always at best simply grasping at the truth, for, as the prophet Isaiah reminds us, God's ways are not our ways, neither are his thoughts our thoughts. Thank God for this day that reminds us of this simple inescapable fact, and use it to deepen your faith and enrich your experience of his living, loving, and transforming presence.

Hymn *Be still, for the presence of the Lord*
The King is among us

Prayer

Almighty and everlasting God,
we are here before you.
Grant us a glimpse of your awesome presence,
and help us to worship you with reverent praise.

Father God,
  we are here before you.
Grant us a sense of your everlasting arms
  surrounding us,
  and help us to trust always in your loving purpose.
Lord Jesus Christ,
  we are here before you.
Grant us grace to hear your call,
  and help us to follow in your footsteps
  wherever that might lead.
Holy Spirit,
  we are here before you.
Grant us openness of heart, mind and spirit,
  and help us to know your peace and power.
Almighty and everlasting God,
  Father, Son and Holy Spirit,
  we are here before you.
Grant that we may know you better,
  and help us to live and work for you,
  this day and always.
Amen.

Slides and music

The Mirror of the Trinity (Magnificat) Praetorius
during which John 15:12-27 is read

Meditation of John

I didn't know what he was on about at the time,
  not the faintest idea,
  despite the way I nodded
  and attempted to smile in the right places.
The Advocate?
The Son who comes from the Father?
What did it all mean?
We believed he was sent by God, yes –
  called to reveal his will,
  build his kingdom –
  but was he saying more,
  pointing to a closer relationship?
It seemed so,
  yet, try as we might, we just couldn't get our heads round it.

'The Lord our God is one' –
isn't that what we'd always been told?
Indeed, he said it himself,
made no bones about it,
so how could he also tell us, 'He who has seen me
has seen the Father'?
We were baffled, there's no other word for it,
and when he went on to talk about the Spirit of truth,
the one his Father would send in his name,
quite simply, by then, we were reeling,
unable to make head or tail of what he was getting at.
'Do we understand now, though?' you ask.
Well, no, we don't actually –
funnily enough if we try to explain it
we still struggle as much as ever;
the more we try, the worse the knots we tie ourselves in.
Yet, strange though it may sound, it makes sense despite that –
for day after day, year after year, we've tasted the truth,
the reality of Father, Son and Holy Spirit.
We look up,
to the stars and the sky,
the wonder of the heavens,
and God is there, enthroned in splendour,
sovereign over all.
We look around,
at the world he's given –
its awesome beauty,
its endless interest,
its bountiful provision –
and he is there,
stretching out his hand in love,
inviting us to share in its wonder.
We look nearby,
at family and friends,
beyond, to the nameless faces of the multitude,
and he is there,
giving and receiving,
waiting to feed and to be fed.
We look within,
at our aching souls,
our pleading hearts,
and he is there,

breathing new life,
new purpose within us.
One God, yes,
but a God we meet in different guises,
different ways,
three in one and one in three.
It sounds odd, I know,
and take it from me, you'll never explain it,
no matter how you try,
yet don't worry, for what finally matters is this:
though words may fail you, the experience never will!

Silence

Slides and music

He was despised and rejected (Messiah) Handel
during which Matthew 13:54-58 is read

Meditation of a resident of Nazareth

Do you know what they're saying about him?
You're not going to believe it!
There are all kinds of rumours flying about –
that he's Moses, Elijah or another of the prophets –
but some are now actually claiming he's the Messiah,
the one we've waited for all this time,
God's promised deliverer!
I said you wouldn't believe it, didn't I?
Yet plenty do, apparently,
a great multitude always around him,
hanging on to his every word,
applauding his every action,
following his every move with open adulation.
And the worst of it is he's done nothing to discourage them,
no attempt whatsoever to cool their ardour a little
or prompt a moment's reasoned reflection.
I'd swear he's coming to believe what they're saying about him,
allowing the hype and hysteria to go to his head –
at least that's how it seemed the other day
when he strolled back here into Nazareth,
entourage in tow.
Barely back five minutes,
and there he was in the synagogue

interpreting the scriptures,
telling us how we should live our lives,
as though he was an expert or something,
privy to some special relationship with God denied the rest of us.
Well, he may have fooled others,
but he didn't fool us –
no chance of pulling the wool over *our* eyes.
We've watched him grow up, you see,
followed his progress
from when he was a bundle in his mother's arms,
and we knew exactly who we were dealing with.
Oh, he'd always been a nice enough lad, I'm not denying that,
never any trouble like some I might mention,
but he was just an ordinary young man,
Jesus the carpenter's son,
from the back streets of Nazareth,
a local boy with, let's face it, dubious origins to put it kindly.
No, I won't go into that,
hardly fair to stir up old dirt,
but you get my drift, don't you?
We knew all about this man the crowds were flocking to,
and, frankly, the idea of him being sent by God was laughable.
The proof was in the pudding,
for what did he actually do here when it came down to it? –
precious few of those signs and wonders
everyone was raving about –
and, quite frankly, after all the hullabaloo
we felt he was a bit of a let-down.
It's strange, though, for no one else has said that,
not to my knowledge, anyway.
I hear fresh reports about him day after day,
and always it's the same story –
healing the sick,
cleansing lepers,
even raising the dead.
Funny he couldn't do it here.
There must be an answer somewhere, mustn't there?
Probably right under my nose if only I could see it.
But it's no good – we know the truth, don't we?
We've seen it with our own eyes,
so, whatever else, the fault can't lie with us.
It can't, can it?

Silence

Hymn *All creatures of our God and King*
Father, we adore you

Slides and music

Cum Sancto Spiritu (Mass in B minor) J. S. Bach
during which Acts 1:15-26 is read

Meditation of Matthias

Did it go to my head, becoming an apostle like that?
Well, yes, I think it possibly did,
for a time anyway.
It was a rare honour, after all,
the ultimate accolade,
so undoubtedly there was a certain swagger in my step
for those first few days;
I'd hardly have been human if there hadn't been.
But it didn't last long,
for I soon came to realise that, if *I* had my role,
others had theirs,
just as important,
just as necessary to the work of the kingdom.
It wasn't a question of us and them,
the select few lording it over the many –
we were part of a team,
each with our own gifts to contribute,
our own strengths and our own weaknesses,
each depending on the other, as Christ depended on us.
We did try putting labels on people for a time, it's true –
deacons, teachers, prophets, apostles –
but it didn't work,
for though the ministries were real enough,
the Spirit couldn't be tied down to them,
neatly pigeon-holed for our convenience.
He was working through all, irrespective of our boundaries,
now here,
now there,
each day new surprises forcing us to think again,
new evidence of his power
compelling us to take stock and broaden our horizons.

It was true for me as much as anyone,
perhaps more than most,
for I had imagined that day when the lot fell on me
that I was someone special,
my name destined to go down in history alongside the greats,
but the truth was soon to dawn
that through Christ times had changed.
We were all special, every one of us,
all called to share in his ministry
to continue his work –
a priesthood of believers,
a company of saints,
the body of Christ.
I wasn't to be a star after all,
but it didn't matter –
how could it, so long as Christ was proclaimed
and his love made known?
What counted, then as now, is that I did my bit,
and that you do yours.

Silence

Slides and music

Salut d'Amour Elgar, during which 1 John 4:7-21 is read

Meditation of John

Sentimental rubbish, that's what some will accuse me of,
another airy-fairy spiel about 'love',
whatever that's supposed to mean.
And I can see their point,
for we do use the word loosely,
enough sometimes to cover a multitude of sins.
Yet I'm sorry, but when it comes to God
there's no other word that will do,
for God *is* love!
It's as simple,
as straightforward,
as uncomplicated as that –
the one description that says it all,
and if you lose that simple truth, you lose everything.
Not that you'd think it, mind you, to hear some people talk,
the picture they paint altogether different.

A God of wrath, they say,
of justice, righteousness, punishment,
sometimes jealous,
often forbidding,
remote, holy, set apart.
He *is* those, of course –
or at least he can be when necessary –
but never out of malice,
only in love.
He longs to bless, not punish,
to give, rather than take away;
his nature is always to have mercy,
to show kindness,
to fill our lives with good things.
If you see him otherwise,
as some vengeful ogre intent on destroying you,
then you don't know him,
for I tell you, God *is* love –
all the law,
all the commandments,
all our faith summed up in that small but wonderful word.
And though I can't put it into words,
you'll understand what I mean if you *do* know him,
for his love will flow in you, through you and from you,
touching every part of your life.
No, we don't deserve such goodness,
not for a moment,
for we'll continue to fail him,
our love always imperfect;
but isn't that just the point,
the thing which makes love so special?
It *does* cover a multitude of sins! –
cleansing,
renewing,
restoring,
forgiving –
refusing to let go come what may.
That's the God we serve,
the sort of being he is –
and if that isn't love, I don't know what is!

Silence

Prayer

Gracious God,
there are some experiences
which we cannot put into words
however hard we try –
moments of joy, love, awe, hope, beauty
and so many more.
Yet though these may defy expression,
they are no less real;
on the contrary they are often more real
and special than any.
So it is with our experience of you.
Together with your Church across the ages,
we strive to articulate our faith,
to describe somehow
everything that you mean to us –
your awesome sovereignty,
your unfailing care,
your intimate closeness,
your presence within –
yet the language we use
seems hopelessly inadequate.
Father, Son and Holy Spirit,
three in one and one in three.
It makes no sense according to human logic,
yet we know it to be true,
not in our minds but in our hearts.
And so we rejoice,
and acknowledge you as our God
in joyful worship,
one God, world without end.
Amen.

Hymn *Father in heaven*
Father, we love you

Blessing

Music *En Trinitatis Speculum (Magnificat)* Praetorius

VISUAL RESOURCES

The following collections of slides have all been used in conjunction with the meditations, readings and music offered in this book. Most powerful of all has been the pack of 144 slides in six sets based on the television series *Jesus of Nazareth* directed by Franco Zeffirelli, produced by the Bible Society.

Sadly, this and many of the other collections referred to here are no longer available from the producers, but the details given may be of help in tracing them, either through your local Diocesan Religious Studies Resource Centre if you have one or, perhaps, through a local library, school, college or university. Failing that, you might try:

Rickett Educational Media Ltd, Great Western House, Langport, Somerset TA10 9YU (01458 253636)

(Note: An asterisk indicates that the resource is no longer commercially available)

*Jesus of Nazareth 1: Jesus – Birth and childhood**
*Jesus of Nazareth 2: Jesus – Begins his ministry**
*Jesus of Nazareth 3: Jesus – Heals**
*Jesus of Nazareth 4: Jesus – Cares**
*Jesus of Nazareth 5: Jesus – In the last week**
*Jesus of Nazareth 6: Jesus – Trial to Resurrection**

Colour transparencies from the TV series directed by Franco Zeffirelli. Was produced by The Bible Society.

*In the Beginning**
A cartoon slide set produced in conjunction with a Ladybird Bible Book primarily aimed at children. Was produced by Scripture Union.

The Life of Christ – I-IV
Slides focusing on the annunciation, nativity, and childhood of Jesus, as 'seen through the eyes of the artist', produced by:

Visual Publications
The Green, Northleach, Cheltenham, Gloucestershire GL54 3EX
Tel 01451 860519

*Come, let us adore**

A series of 27 slides on the nativity. Was produced by Audio Visual Productions UK.

Oberammergau 1990

A sequence of 36 slides from the Oberammergau Passion Plays, produced by:

Huber
Drosselstraße 7, D-8100 Garmisch-Partenkirchen, Germany

Man of the Cross

A slide-sound presentation (code: 70P326), also available as a set of 15 posters (code 73P262), using a variety of artistic media, including photography, vividly portraying the Way of the Cross. Produced by:

St Paul MultiMedia Productions
199 Kensington High Street, London W8 6BA
Tel 020 7937 9591

*He Carries Our Cross**

An audiovisual programme for liturgy, prayer and reflection, including slides of line-sketches, focusing on the events of the Passion under two subsections: (a) Journey to Jerusalem, and (b) Journey to the Cross. Was produced by St Paul MultiMedia Productions.

*Bread and Wine**

Pictures of the elements of the Eucharist, particularly suitable for meditations on the Last Supper. Was produced for the Church Pastoral Aid Society by Falcon Audio Visual Aids.

*St Paul**

A radiovision slideset consisting of 45 picture slides. Was produced by the BBC.

*The Story of St Paul**

A picture slideset produced in conjunction with a Ladybird Bible Book primarily aimed at children. Was produced by Ladybird Books.

*The Gospel: Life of Jesus**

A cartoon slideset. Was produced by St Paul MultiMedia Productions.